CCNP R[illegible]
Swi[illegible]ng

Secrets To Acing The Exam
and
Successful Finding And Landing Your Next CCNP Routing and Switching Certified Job

Write a review to receive any *FREE* eBook from our Catalogue - $99 Value!

If you recently bought this book we would love to hear from you! Benefit from receiving a free eBook from our catalogue at http://www.emereo.org/ if you write a review on Amazon (or the online store where you purchased this book) about your last purchase!

How does it work?

To post a review on Amazon, just log in to your account and click on the Create your own review button (under Customer Reviews) of the relevant product page. You can find examples of product reviews in Amazon. If you purchased from another online store, simply follow their procedures.

What happens when I submit my review?

Once you have submitted your review, send us an email at review@emereo.org with the link to your review, and the eBook you would like as our thank you from http://www.emereo.org/. Pick any book you like from the catalogue, up to $99 RRP. You will receive an email with your eBook as download link. It is that simple!

This book figures out ways to boil down critical exam and job landing concepts into real world applications and scenarios. Which makes this book user-friendly, interactive, and valuable as a resource long after students pass the exam. People who teach CCNP Routing and Switching classes for a living or for their companies understand the true value of this book. You certainly will too.

To Prepare for the exam this book tells you:

- What you need to know about the CCNP Routing and Switching Certification and exam
- Preparation Tips for passing the CCNP Routing and Switching Certification Exam
- Taking tests

The book contains several suggestions on how preparing yourself for an interview. This is an aspect that many people underestimate, whilst having a well-written CV, a personal blog, and possibly a number of past projects is definitively important - there is much more to prepare for. It covers non-technical aspects (how to find a job, resume, behavioral etc.). A 'Must-study' before taking a Tech Interview.

To Land the Job, it gives you the hands-on and how-to's insight on

- Typical CCNP Routing and Switching Careers
- Finding Opportunities - the best places to find them
- Writing Unbeatable Resumes and Cover Letters
- Acing the Interview
- What to Expect From Recruiters
- How employers hunt for Job-hunters.... and More

This book offers excellent, insightful advice for everyone from entry-level to senior professionals. None of the other such career guides compare with this one.

It stands out because it:

- Explains how the people doing the hiring think, so that you can win them over on paper and then in your interview
- Is filled with useful work-sheets
- Explains every step of the job-hunting process - from little-known ways for finding openings to getting ahead on the job

This book covers everything. Whether you are trying to get your first CCNP Routing and Switching Job or move up in the system, you will be glad you got this book.

Contents

Cisco Career Certifications

Cisco Career Certifications

Cisco Career Certifications are IT Professional certifications for Cisco Systems products. The tests are administered by Pearson VUE. The five levels of certification are Entry Associate Professional Expert and Architect along with targeted certifications for Specialist and Technician. These are obtainable in seven dissimilar subject areas Routing Switching Design Network Security Service Provider Storage Networking Voice and Wireless.

education

The traditional educational establishment that teaches Cisco skills is called the Cisco Networking Academy. 1 Cisco Networking Academy students can demand examination vouchers that let them to get a needed examination over an extended time of time. 2 Cisco courses are also offered at collegiate institutions and education is obtainable from Cisco Learning Partners such as the Cisco 360 Learning Program for CCIE and the Cisco Learning Network.

Certification

The table below shows the dissimilar paths and levels for CISCO certifications. To really get CISCO cert exams you must discover a test centre who works with Pearson Vue. Cisco says there are no prerequisites for CCIE exams but they are written exams and they commend lots of practice. There is also a hands on lab test. Both the written and lab tests are USD. Please annotation that Senior Associate is not an functionary CISCO level but the Network Security Voice and Wireless paths all use CCNA as a prerequisite. CISCO lists them at the same associate level as a CCNA.

Certification Paths
Level Routing Switching 3 Storage Networking 4 Service Provider 5 Design 6 Network Security 7 Voice 8 Wireless 9
Professional CCNP 642 901 BSCI 642 812 BCMSN or 642 892 Composite 642 825 ISCW 642 845 ONT CCIP 642 901 BSCI or 642 892 Composite 642 642 QOS 642 661 BGP 642 611 MPLS or 642 691 BGP

+ MPLS CCDP 642 901 BSCI 642 812 BCMSN or 642 892 Composite 642 873 ARCH CCSP 642 504 SNRS 642 524 SNAF 642 533 IPS 642 591 CANAC or 642 545 MARS or 642 515 SNAA CCNA Security CCVP 642 642 QoS 642 436 CVOICE 642 426 TUC Communications Manager itinerary 642 446 CIPT1 642 456 CIPT2 or CallManager itinerary 642 444 CIPT 4. 1 642 453 GWGK any CCIE Certification or a sound CCNA Voice CCNP Wireless 642 731 CUWSS 642 741 IUWVN 642 746 IUWMS 642 736 IAUWS any CCIE Certification or a sound CCNA Wireless
Senior Associate

CCDA 640 863 DESGN CCNA and BCMSN level information to succeed the cert examination. CCNA Security 640 553 IINS a sound CCNA CCNA Voice 640 460 IIUC or 642 436 CVOICE 6. 0 a sound CCNA or any CCIE Certification CCNA Wireless 640 721 IUWNE a sound CCNA
Associate CCNA 640 802 CCNA or 640 822 ICND1 640 816 ICND2 | Entry Level CCENT 640 822 ICND1
10

Re certification

All CCENT CCNA CCDA CCNP CCDP CCSP CCVP CCNA Security CCNA Voice CCNA Wireless CCIP CCIE certifications and Specialist certifications are sound for 3 years. Re certification requires re taking the examination or passing a higher level test. 11 12

Entry level certification

The lowest level of certification is Cisco Certified Entry Networking Technician CCENT which covers fundamental networking information. It is appropriate for an entryway level net support situation. CCENT certified personnel can set up control and troubleshoot a small undertaking net including fundamental net security. 13 CCENT is the first pace towards a CCNA certification. The CCENT certification is earned upon passing the Interconnecting Cisco Networking Devices Part 1 ICND1 Exam 640 822.

Associate certifications

Associate Certifications is the 2nd level of certifications. Associate Certifications split separate certifications by subject substance.

Cisco Certified Network Associate

The Cisco Certified Network Associate CCNA certification covers skills necessary to administer devices on small or intermediate state sized networks. 14 This certification requires the ICND1 640 822 and ICND2 640 816 exams. Examinees may get the exams separately or the composite 640 802 CCNA examination. 15 It is generally a prerequisite to more advanced certifications such as the CCNA specialty exams and Cisco Professional level certifications e. g. CCNP CCNP Wireless CCNP Security etcetera.

These exams are conducted by Pearson VUE test centers. 16

Specialty Paths

CCNA certified individuals specialize by engineering. All specialized tracks require passing and maintain a CCNA certification.

Security

CCNA Security validates information of security framework threats and vulnerabilities to networks and source of danger mitigation. Required skills comprise installation troubleshooting and monitoring of net devices to maintain the moral soundness confidentiality and availability of data and devices. This certification is earned by passing the IINS 640 553 Implementing Cisco IOS Network Security or IINS examination. 17 18 The IINS 640 554 examination is needed for continuing the security certification itinerary to the CCNP.

Voice

The CCNA Voice certification validates skills for ability to speak technologies such as ability to speak technologies administrator ability to speak applied technologist and ability to speak manager. The certification involves implementing Cisco IOS Unified Communications. It validates skills in VoIP technologies such as IP PBX IP telephony handset phone call discipline in personal activities and ability to speak earth mail solutions. Candidates acquire vulnerability to the elements to the Cisco Unified Communications architectonics and design that cover mobility comportment and TelePresence applications. 19 20 640 461 ICOMM V8. 0 Introducing Cisco Voice and Unified Communications Administration is the needed examination.

Wireless

The CCNA Wireless certification covers wireless LANs including networking associates administrators wireless support specialists and WLAN project managers. The certification validates skills in the configuration implementation and support of wireless LANs. 640 721 IUWNE Implementing Cisco Unified Wireless Networking Essentials is the needed examination.

Service provider

CCNA Service Provider focuses validates the way to configure and implement baseline Cisco Service Provider Next Generation networks. The needed Exams are 640 875 Building Cisco Service Provider Next Generation Networks Part 1 SPNGN1 and 640 878 Building Cisco Service Provider Next Generation Networks Part 2 SPNGN2. Standard CCNA certification is not a prerequisite. The grade Building Cisco Service Provider Next Generation Networks is delivered in two parts.

Part 1 is a 5 day instructor led track that supplies the fundamental information and skills necessary to support a service provider net. The track supplies information of the enormous net parts and helps learners to comprehend how service provider networks work. The track introduces IP Next Generation Network IP NGN architectonics. The track also comprises of remote labs that support benefit concerned with actual use or practice skills for deploying fundamental Cisco IOS IOS XE and Cisco IOS XR software features. Part 2 is a 5 day instructor led track that supplies information of net construction and IP NGN architectonics. The track comprises of additional remote labs. 21

Service provider operations

CCNA service provider operations supplies skills in a prescriptive troubleshooting environment in a carrier grade IP NGN center net framework. The needed exams are 640 822 ICND1 Interconnecting Cisco Networking Devices Part 1 ICND1 and 640 760 SSPO Supporting Cisco Service Provider IP NGN Operations SSPO. 22

Cisco Certified Design Associate

Cisco Certified Design Associate CCDA certified engineers can design switched or routed networks of LANs WANs and broadband services. CCNA is not needed to get the CCDA examination 640

864 DESGN but Cisco recommends being well known with CCNA level matter as well as BCMSN or SWITCH level information of Cisco based LANs. 23

Professional certifications

Cisco Certified Network Professional CCNP certification validates information and skills needed to set up configure and troubleshoot converged local and wide field networks with 100 to 500 or more end devices. A sound CCNA certification is needed to obtain a CCNP certification. 24 25

Network Professional

The CCNP validates the way to design implement verify and troubleshoot local and wide field undertaking networks and work collaboratively with specialists on advanced security ability to speak wireless and video recording solutions. In improver to CCNA exams professionals must succeed three independent professional person level exams. The certification track changed in July 2010 with various movement from one country to another paths obtainable for those that had begun but not completed the CCNP certification process.

Required exams

642 902 ROUTE Implementing Cisco IP Routing ROUTE 26
642 813 SWITCH Implementing Cisco IP Switched Networks SWITCH 27
642 832 TSHOOT Troubleshooting and Maintaining Cisco IP Networks TSHOOT 28

Design Professional

With a CCDP certification a net professional person can talk about design and make advanced addressing and routing security net management data centre and IP multicast undertaking architectures that comprise virtual personal networking and wireless domains. An vigorous CCDA certification is a prerequisite for this certification.

Required exams

642 902 ROUTE Implementing Cisco IP Routing ROUTE 26

642 813 SWITCH Implementing Cisco IP Switched Networks SWITCH 27
642 874 ARCH Designing Cisco Network Service Architecture 29
Note that 642 902 ROUTE and 642 813 SWITCH are also needed for CCNP. After passing CCNP and CCDA CCDP requires only 642 873 ARCH.

Internetwork Professional

The CCIP certification shall go into retirement start October 29 2012. 30 It shall be replaced by the CCNP Service Provider certification.

Internetwork Professional Service Provider

The CCNP Service Provider certification replaced the retiring CCIP certification.

Required exams

642 883 SPROUTE Deploying Cisco Service Provider Network Routing
642 885 SPADVROUTE Deploying Cisco Service Provider Advanced Routing
642 887 SPCORE Implementing Cisco Service Provider Next Generation Core Network Services
642 889 SPEDGE Implementing Cisco Service Provider Next Generation Edge Network Services
Security

Formerly Cisco Certified Security Professional CCSP.

The CCNP Security certification software is aligned to the job part of the Cisco Network Security Engineer accountable for security in routers switches networking devices and appliances as well as choosing deploying supporting and troubleshooting firewalls VPNS and IDS IPS solutions for their networking environments. The CCNP Security certification requires CCNA Security or any CCIE Certification.

CCNP Security exams and recommended education

642 637 SECURE v1. 0 Secure v1. 0 Securing Networks with Cisco Routers and Switches SECURE v1. 0
642 618 FIREWALL v2. 0 Deploying Cisco ASA Firewall Solutions FIREWALL v2. 0

642 648 VPN v2. 0 Deploying Cisco ASA VPN Solutions VPN v2. 0
642 627 IPS v7. 0
Voice

Formerly Cisco Certified Voice Professional CCVP.

The Cisco Certified Network Professional for Voice CCNP Voice certification validates the skills needed to influence the correct engineering and solutions for making safe networks. With it a net professional person can march in protest the skills needed to implement and control net infrastructures to supply unified communications services. The course of academic program emphasizes Cisco Router IOS and Catalyst Switch UC features. CCNA Voice certification is a prerequisite. 31 32

Required exams

642 437 CVOICE v8. 0 Implementing Cisco Voice Communications and QoS Implementing Cisco Unified Communications
642 447 CIPT1 v8. 0 Implementing Cisco Unified Communications Part 1
642 457 CIPT2 v8. 0 Implementing Cisco Unified Communications Part 2
642 427 TVOICE v8. 0 Troubleshooting Cisco Unified Communications
642 467 CAPPS v8. 0 Integrating Cisco Unified Communications Applications
Wireless

CCNP Wireless covers all aspects of wireless networking principles and hypothesis. This certification requires four tests that cover Wireless Site Survey Wireless Voice Networks Wireless Mobility Services and Wireless Security. The prerequisite is a sound CCNA Wireless certification.

Required exams

642 731 CUWSS Conducting Cisco Unified Wireless Site Survey CUWSS
642 741 IUWVN Implementing Cisco Unified Wireless Voice Networks IUWVN
642 746 IUWMS Implementing Cisco Unified Wireless Mobility Services IUWMS
642 736 IAUWS Implementing Advanced Cisco Unified Wireless Se-

curity IAUWS
Expert level certifications

Cisco Certified Design Expert

CCDE runs in analog with the more accepted CCIE software in some areas providing a higher skill set than CCIE. Specifically CCDE identifies net professionals who have expert net design skills. Network design translates organization requirements into end to end net designs and a solutions access to net enlargement and unification. 33 CCDE focuses on net architectonics and does not cover implementation and operations. CCDE supplies a vendor of no distinctive quality course of academic program testing organization requirements test design planning and validation practices. 34 The track came about because employers needed a manner to name knowledgeable net designers and architects who could place where a person or organization can be found all aspects of existing and fresh networking technologies and trends. 35 While engineers including many CCIEs had been fulfilling this part certification had not advanced beyond the CCDP certification. CCDE numbering adopts a dissimilar data data formatting than CCIE and appears to be break open into a yr and numeral in that yr. The same CCIE tools are being used to verify meeting the standards and requirements status. CCDE certified individuals can use CCIE accomplishment exams to re certify and vice versa. CCDE supplies advanced net framework design principles and fundamentals for big networks. A CCDE can march in protest an way to invent solutions which place where a person or organization can be found planning design unification optimization operations security and ongoing support focused at the framework level.

Cisco Certified Internetwork Expert

Cisco Certified Internetwork Expert is Cisco's highest certification consisting of six tracks. As of October 6 2010 there were 25,810 people with vigorous CCIE certifications. 36 37 38 From 2002 to 2005 39 it was voted as such clarification needed in CertCities periodic publication. It was voted the most technically advanced IT certification by CertMag 40 and is generally reported as the highest salaried certification in IT salary surveys.

CCIE began in 1993 41 originally with a two day lab later changing to a one day data data formatting. Fewer than 3 of Cisco certified individuals attain CCIE certification and on average expend thousands of dollars and 18 months studying before passing. 42 Many candidates make education labs at native using previous equipment then exchange for money it to another candidates after passing. Alternatively candidates may hire framework for holding objects time online. The CCIE consists of a written examination and a lab examination in each track. The written examination is a prerequisite of the lab examination and has a cost of $ 350 per attempt. The written examination consists of 100 questions that must be completed in 2 hours. Upon passing the written examination the nominee has eighteen months to get the lab examination. The nominee has three years after passing the written examination to successfully having every necessary part the lab. The lab is an eight hour hands on examination designed to march in protest that the nominee knows Internetworking hypothesis and shows advanced hands on mastery. Candidates that do not succeed the CCIE lab in that interval must re succeed the written examination before again attempting the CCIE lab examination. The minimal waiting time between attempts is one calendar month.

As of 2012 the CCIE Lab costs $ 1500 per attempt and is offered at ten Cisco locations worldwide. Some CCIE tracks are not offered at all ten. According to a Cisco inspect the average cost to prepare for CCIE certification was $ 9050 as of April 2006 spent mostly on practice equipment and research matter. 43 There are no traditional prerequisites for the CCIE written examination but Cisco recommends at least 3 5 years networking practice. CCIE was the first Cisco Certified accomplishment and no another certifications were previously obtainable. The associate and professional person certifications recognized the fact that CCIE is overkill for many networking personnel. Cisco has chosen not to make lower level certifications prerequisites for the CCIE certification.

It is possible to book several CCIE certifications. As of September 9 2008 1,729 individuals held several CCIE certifications. Of those 274 book three or more CCIE certifications. 44 This accomplishment was cited as essentially a PhD in the internet by Adam McCombs in Season 1 Episode 10 of Shark Tank.

CCIE Numbering and Recertification

Upon successful completion of the lab examination a fresh CCIE is awarded a CCIE numeral. The first CCIE numeral allocated in 1993 was 1,024 and expanded thereafter. As of August 2011 the highest CCIE numeral allocated was only over 30,000. The first numeral was allocated to the first CCIE lab location rather than to an personal and was featured as a plaque at the entrance to the lab. Number 1025 was awarded to Stuart Biggs who created the first written examination and first lab examination. The first individual to succeed both CCIE written and lab exams was Terry Slattery 45 who was consulting at Cisco when the lab was devised. Slattery was the first CCIE who was not an worker of Cisco. 46 47 Each CCIE retains their numeral regardless of how many certifications he or she receives. Every two years a CCIE has to get a written test to keep in one's mind the certification. If this is not achieved the certification is suspended. After one further yr without passing the certification is revoked. The certification can then only be regained by starting from scrape. Recertification can occur up to 2 years before the expiration day of the month. After certification recertification a CCIE must stay in one place and anticipate something 6 months before re certifying.

CCIE examination paths

Routing Switching

Routing and Switching is by afar the most well-known track with 35,272 worldwide certified individuals as of May 18 2012. 48 The certification covers a diversity of networking concepts and protocols.

Security

The Security track covers advanced subjects in subjects such as ASA IDS IOS security and many others.

Service Provider

The Service Provider track covers advanced subjects in Optical networks DSL WAN switching Voice over IP Content networking Broadband Cable and Metro Ethernet.

Voice

The Voice track covers advanced subjects in subjects such as Quality of Service MGCP Call Manager Cisco's VoIP PBX Cisco Unity Connection Cisco's Voice Messaging platform Unity Express Unified Contact Center Express Cisco Unified Presence Server Cisco's HWIC 4ESW and the 3750 24PS. Only 802 CCIE Voice certified engineers were nowadays as of September 9 2008. Most candidates succeed after three or four lab attempts but some have needed more than six. The lab examination is reputed to be as much a test of time management and planning as of technical expertness. What sets the Voice lab examination apart from another CCIE lab exams is the widely dissimilar platforms that are being used. Configurations have to be achieved on the Windows 2003 Server environment a CallManager web based GUI and the IOS command row. As such it involves a great deal of reverse and forth small grained or smooth tuning between the numerous platforms.

Storage Networking

CCIE Storage Networking validates expert level information of intelligent storage solutions using several shipping options over lengthy distances.

Wireless

Candidates who succeed the CCIE Wireless certification exams march in protest broad theoretical information of wireless networking and a entirely of one substance with no holes inside know-how of wireless local field networking WLAN technologies from Cisco.

Service Provider Operations

CCIE Service Provider Operations candidates must demonstrate expert skills in troubleshooting and maintain complicated service provider IP NGN center PE PE and PE CE net infrastructures in both IOS and IOS XR operating environments.

Data Center

Cisco has announced the September availability of a CCIE Data Center certification 49 which certifies the expert level skills needed to design prepare operate check and troubleshoot complicated data centre networks. The CCIE Data Center written examination shall be obtainable Sept. 3 2012 50 the lab examination is expected to be obtainable in October. 51 Cisco has not announced corresponding Associate or Professional level certifications.

Retired CCIE tracks

Some previously awarded CCIE specializations have been no longer active in your work by Cisco. These are

WAN Switching CCIE Essentially a specialisation focusing on the IGX BPX change one thing for another products which had been acquired as portion of the StrataCom possession
ISP Dial CCIE
SNA IP Integration CCIE aka CCIE Blue
Design CCIE NOTE The CCIE Design and CCDE are completely dissimilar design tests in data data formatting and subjects examined
People who book these presently no longer active in your work certifications can stay behind CCIE's provided they continue to get recertification exams. They presently book the title of respect CCIE rather than CCIE Security or some another specialization.

Architect

The Cisco Certified Architect CCAr certification assesses the practice and competency of net designers who can support the increasingly complicated networks of worldwide organizations and effectively interpret in another language organization strategies into technical strategies. 52 53

Certification Process

The Cisco Certified Architect certification is administered as a committee having supervisory powers examination.
Candidates propose and protect an architectonics resolution to a set of organization requirements. Candidates are asked to modify their proposals on the travel through the be airborne based on additional requirements presented by the committee having supervisory powers.
Prerequisites comprise a CCDE certification approximately 10 years of industry practice and favorable reception into the software via an application process.
Responsibilities

Responsibilities of the Cisco Certified Architect

Lead creative activity and phylogenesis of undertaking architectonics
Analyze engineering and industry commercial trends
Establish governing principles for Enterprise networks
Selection of engineering and products
Identification of organization resource needs
Lead the growth of information exchange and knowledge transfer

design for undertaking net architectonics
Technician

Cisco Certified Technicians have the skills to diagnose fix repair and substitute for a defective or inadequate one tending to find errors and flaws Cisco networking and system devices at client sites. Technicians work closely with the Cisco Technical Assistance Center TAC to quickly and efficiently resolve support incidents. 54

As of April 2012 there were three domains obtainable for CCT certification

CCT Routing and Switching
CCT Data Center
CCT Telepresence
Specialist

In improver to the broad certifications above Cisco also supplies dozens of Specialist certifications. 55 These exams are frequently focused on particular engineering and generally targeted at members of the Cisco Partner Program including those selling designing or supporting Cisco products and services. By combining various exams a Cisco cooperator can benefit specialty status and thus live up to for additional cooperator benefits. 56

Retired certifications

Over time as technologies change and products are made obsolete some certifications are no longer active in your work. Retired certifications are no longer sound.

Certifications that drop into this general concept are listed below.

Cisco education and Certification Paths

Cisco education and Certification Paths

Cisco is one of the biggest Enterprise Networking and Service Providers of routers and switches wireless systems security systems ability to speak and communications engineering. With increasing use of Cisco Network engineering and Infrastructures the need of Cisco certification for IT professionals is at its all time highest point.

Whether you are a recently or harvested grad knowledgeable IT professional person or thinking of a vocation change taking Cisco education and IT Professional Certifications validates your skills to give a performance a diversity of IT functions and ensures to your potentiality employers that you have the concerned with actual use or practice education of working with routers and switches net security to implementing wireless and unified communications.

There are seven dissimilar paths of Cisco education certification Routing and Switching Suitable for professionals who set up and support Cisco engineering based networks in which LAN and WAN routers and switches reside. Certifications that can be achieved are CCENT CCNA CCNP and CCIE Routing Switching.

Design This is for professionals who design Cisco engineering based networks in which LAN and WAN routers and switches reside. Certification that can be achieved is CCDA.

Network Security Network professionals who design and implement Cisco Secure networks can take on this Cisco education and certification. Certifications that can be achieved are CCENT CCNA Security CCNP Security and CCIE Security.

Wireless Network professionals who configure implement and support wireless networks should aim for this. Certifications that can be achieved are CCENT CCNA Wireless CCNP Wireless and CCIE Wireless.

Voice Network professionals who set up and maintain Voice solutions over IP networks should move for this itinerary. Certifications that can be achieved are CCENT CCNA Voice CCNP Voice and CCIE Voice.

Storage Networking Suitable for professionals implementing over extended net framework using several shipping options. Certifications that can be achieved are CCENT CCNA CCNP and CCIE Storage Networking.

Service Provider Professionals who work with framework or admittance solutions in a Cisco end to end environment primarily in the telecommunications scene can aim for this. Certifications that can be achieved are CCENT CCNA CCNA Service Provider Operations CCIP Service Provider Operations and CCIE Service Provider Operations.

To acquire measurable returns on your investment on Cisco education you need to discover a good Cisco education Institute. You should think about following qualities of a Cisco education Partner
Authorized Cisco education Partner
Certified Cisco Systems Instructors
Cisco Authorized and Approved Content
Real Cisco Equipment and Hands on Experience
After Course Support

Cisco certificates are the most sought after certificates among networking lovers across the globe.

For more intelligence about Cisco education kindly travel to http www. koenig solutions. com

Preparation Tips For The CCNP Routing and Switching Certification Exam

Exam time Hints for managing tenseness

Exams are a time when tenseness levels are higher than usual. Stress can be confirming helping you to stick stay put motivated and focused. However too much tenseness can be unhelpful it can make you undergo an emotional sensation overwhelmed confused exhausted and edgy. It's significant to adjudicate and hold onto things in perspective and discover ways of reducing tenseness if things appear to be getting on top upper upside of you.

Suggestions for managing examination tenseness

Effective research habits Many people undergo an emotional sensation overwhelmed at examination time having to make revisions to a great deal of intelligence in a having little length space of time and not know-how track matter can be a big tenseness. Check out Exam time Hints for result driven studying for more concerned with actual use or practice proposal for an appropriate course of action on result driven research techniques.

Keep your modus operandi outdoors studying + get steady

breaks It's significant to have steady research breaks and time for absence of tension and physical exercise. Going for a use one's feet to advance be operating or functioning or to the gym is not a waste of time it is a very valuable manner to well defined your top person who is in charge and support you research better.

Watching your pet TV show or going to the movies are also good ways to get a break from studying.

Limit drugs Caffeine Eg beverage no doz V and another drugs Eg travel at an excessive or illegal velocity coke bestow you a having little length elevator before making you cease operating abruptly and cause a sharp or stinging pain. They can make you undergo an emotional sensation ill and unable to slumber or focus one's attention properly. You really research better with steady breaks getting lots of slumber and from exercising really.

Have a numeral of options for the futurity Getting the marks to acquire into your first predisposition is very valuable but it's not the end of the earth if you don't there are another options to acquire into your track. These comprise deferring and getting some concerned with actual use or practice practice in your field doing further research writing to the university retaking some subjects in some cases or transferring in after a yr or two. And if you do agree to another verbal act of offering you may discover that you like it even more.

Manage expectations External pressures around exams can be vast. It can be tough to deal with particularly with kin and people you value but you need to recall that it's your life and your examination with you in discipline in personal activities. Things that might support you control expectations

Base expectations on your earlier than the present time performance and doing the best you can do.

Put the examination in linguistic context of use. In the schema organization of concepts of your life how significant is it If you don't do as well as you'd hoped there are always another alternatives. It's not going to say out loud for the purpose of recording whether you are a good or a below average in quality or defective individual or whether you are a success or failing. Exams can't gauge these sorts of things all they gauge is how well you can being here the matter asked for by the examiner nothing more nothing less.

Take it as a compliment admittedly this can be easier said than achieved. These people need you to do well and consider that you are capable of achieving. Their determination of achieving is sometimes a little or a great deal misguided so you need to educate people about what you consider is realistic. Talk to them discover out what they desire and expectancy for you and recite them what you are thinking and touch sensation.

Use the expectations of yourself and others to assist your studying. Talk to people about how you are touch sensation view if they have any proposal for an appropriate course of action or support they can verbal act of offering. It's significant to inquire for and agree to support from those around particularly kin members.

Look after your body It's simple to let exams acquire on top upper upside of you and to blank draw a fail to remember to see after yourself. If possible adjudicate to acquire a good nights slumber. It's a good time to make an endeavor to take in solid food fit including eating plenty of fruits and vegetables.

Ask for + agree to support If you're touch sensation overwhelmed you might discover it helpful to talking to a instructor or counsellor. It's also significant to inquire for and agree to support from your kin if you can. This support might be concerned with actual use or practice like picking you up from the library or emotional including proposal for an appropriate course of action or support.

Remember. .

There's always a emitting light at the end of the passageway. Exams have a start and an end and the tenseness that goes along with them should end with the examination. Once the paper's in there's nothing more you can do to legally effect of one thing or person the outcome which means it's presently time to chill and enjoy love to do the summertime.

Exam Preparation Tips

For many people examination time is the most stressful portion of the educational institution yr. With so much riding on the outcome there can be a high academic degree of insistency to give a performance well. Here are some examination preparedness tips to support you excel in educational institution.

Getting Started

The earlier you begin the more time you shall have to prepare for the examination. You don't have to stay in one place and anticipate something until examination time approaches adjudicate to set the distinct time period in a sequence of events from the start of the track by reviewing the matter after each grade. By starting early and studying on a steady base you shall have a better opportunity to take suck up the intelligence and life shall be a great deal easier when it's time to put it all together for the examination.

Make sure all of your track matter is well organized so you can discover and fill up any gaps. If you fail to attend an event or activity any classes acquire the notes from your friends correct away instead of scrambling at the terminal unit of time equal to 60 seconds. Proper organization shall support you to acquire a better visual representation of the matter that has to be covered and ameliorate the run of the research process.

Creating a Study Plan

As the examination nears you shall need to make a design to support you research effectively and downplay tenseness. The first pace is to amount of money expressed numerically out how much time and endeavor you must inscribe or address by way of compliment to studying for the examination by asking the following questions

How much matter do you need to cover

How hard is the matter

How much time is obtainable

Do you have any another priorities during the research time

What is the data data formatting of the examination

How significant is the examination

What is your performance mark for the examination

To prepare the research design representation of the earth's surface out all of the matter that has to be covered and make a schedule showing what when and how much you shall research each day. If you have kept up with the track work studying shall involve revision of the matter that you have already covered. If you are behind in the track you shall have to complete the readings and another uncompleted work before starting the revision if there isn't enough time to move over everything you must make up one's mind what is most significant for the examination.

Here are some tips to come after in making your research design

- sum of money allocated your time realistically
- allocate the research time into many manageable research sessions
- split separate the track matter into small segments and assign them to the research sessions
- set well defined and particular goals for the research sessions
- prioritize to make sure that matter weighted more heavily in the examination gets sufficient research time
- get into report your familiarity with the matter and the trouble level
- don't make the research sessions too lengthy
- research sessions should have enough diversity in conditions of subjects and actions to keep from happening boredom and loss of effectiveness
- evade cramming before the examination and
- don't blank draw a fail to remember to comprise steady breaks.

Studying for the Exam

You are presently armed with a design and prepared to begin studying for the examination. Try to research in a point in space where you can focus one's attention and won't be interrupted. You can work with others or join a research group if you discover it helpful but be careful to hold onto it from turning into an inefficient use of your time. Some proven research tools and techniques are listed below people respond to dissimilar learning styles so use what works for you.

Revising with Summary Notes

Make a condensed version of your readings and grade notes by making brief statement notes. Pinpoint the prime conditions and concepts and make sure that you comprehend them. You can name prime conditions and concepts by paying faculty or power of mental concentration to what has been emphasized in your classes textbooks and track syllabus. For instance if a specific topic has taken up a great deal of time in the schoolroom it is more plausible to be on the examination and you should have a good know-how of it.

The process of making brief statement notes can support you to keep in one's mind more intelligence. By writing the intelligence thoughtfully instead of only seeing it you can invent a greater process of perceiving of the matter. To get this further make active your another senses you can recite the brief statement notes aloud and even record and hear to them.

Memorizing with Flashcards

Flashcards or alphabetical listing cards are a good memorization tool. diminish your brief statement notes into projectile points keywords lists formulas and diagrams and place them onto a bill of carte du carte for each topic. Some people like to use flashcards to prepare their brief statement notes in the first place while others discover that it leads to intelligence overload.

The items on the flashcards act as memory triggers. By memorizing the flashcards you can make better or more attractive your way to recall larger bits of intelligence referenced by the triggers. You can carry the cards with you and inspection them even when you have only having little length bursts of time obtainable.

Practicing under Exam Conditions

Knowing the track matter is necessary but not sufficient to warrantee success on the examination you also need to be capable to communicate the answers effectively under examination conditions. Practice using small part representative of the whole questions in the same data data formatting as the examination and respond them in a simulated test environment. The small part representative of the whole questions can be sourced from previous exams and assignments which are frequently like from yr to yr with small changes. Even though you are only practicing it is better to communicate or express by writing complete answers to the questions so you can work via the complete cerebration process.

The practice meeting should attend wait assist as a response iteration. Check the answers to the practice questions to diagnose your strengths and weaknesses. If you are having little physical or spiritual strength in an field move reverse and research it further to place where a person or organization can be found any gaps.

Taking Care of Yourself

Don't blank draw a fail to remember to get tending of yourself during the examination preparedness. It is very significant to be in good mental and involving the body circumstance for the examination. A small amount of tenseness can acquire you psyched but too much mental or involving the body tense up can be harmful to your performance. The terminal thing you need to do is to sabotage your efforts by ignoring your well being.

After you complete studying get some time to loosen unwind. Don't stick stay put up too tardy if you can support it and adjudicate to acquire a good night's slumber. Eat before the examination to make your vigor but evade of great physical weight foods that can make you drowsy.

Keep a confirming mental attitude about the examination. Think of it as a manner to march in protest your information and not as some imposing call into question. Go to the examination focused and relaxed you have achieved the work presently it's time to reap the rewards.

Examination hints

Exam calendar week can be hard unsafe even overwhelming. You may undergo an emotional sensation incapacitated and hopeless as though there is nothing you can do. After a semester of too many classes and too much work you consider you'll have to stick stay put up all dark studying to travel past your final examination exams.

But stay in one place and anticipate something Help is on the manner

Below are my easy to use hints for examination time built during ten arduous years as a learner and fifteen more as a instructor.

Two Weeks Before the Exam

- Make up a set of research sheets for each grade.
- Each set of research sheets should summarize the reading your grade notes and any handouts.
- Type the research sheets so they are easily readable. Use plenty of fearless and daring type and white space to accentuate significant ideas.
- For the next two weeks interpret something via your research sheets three times each day. Do not adjudicate tough to memorize the intelligence. Just interpret something the notes once three times per day.

The Night Before the Exam

- Read your research sheets as usual.
- Go to bed early and acquire a good night's slumber.

The Day of the Exam

- Set your alarm clock and acquire up early. Allow plenty of time to acquire to the examination.
- Eat a good morning meal including easy sugars ripened reproductive body of a seed plant juice complicated carbohydrates breakfast food or bread and protein milk eggs flesh of animals dairy. This shall support your blood refined sugar stick stay put at a horse barn level and since your grey matter runs on refined sugar you don't need to have an empty army armored combat vehicle.
- Caffeine has been shown to augment alertness and performance. If you are a habitual client of caffeine be sure to acquire your accustomed portion of medicine.
- Take along a part of ripened reproductive body of a seed plant to take in solid food during the examination. This shall support hold onto your blood refined sugar even so you don't hoop covering a wheel during the second 50 percent of the examination time.

During the Exam

- If you undergo an emotional sensation in a state of physical or nervous tension loosen unwind get a having great spatial extension downward breath and recall that you see the matter because you've been reviewing for two weeks.

- Keep your organ of sight on the timepiece while taking the examination. Allow enough time to complete the complete test. Avoid focusing on one query and running out of time on others.
- Read the complete examination before start to communicate or express by writing. Know your hostile people in another words.
- Be sure your title is on the test. This sounds silly but sometimes if we undergo an emotional sensation in a state of physical or nervous tension or pressured we blank draw a fail to remember the little things.
- Read each query a second time then respond that query.
- Go on to the next query. Remember to see at the timepiece and hold onto arousing deep emotion via the test.
- After the first 60 period of time and fifteen minutes loosen unwind stretch extend one's limbs take in solid food your ripened reproductive body of a seed plant. Calm down. You see the matter.
- Use the complete examination time rather than rushing via the test.

Special Information for Students Taking Essay Exams

- Read the query carefully and analyze what the instructor wants in the respond. If the query has many parts use these parts to structure your respond.
- Use the writing process sudden insight bring order and organization to linear boundary total supporting intelligence communicate or express by writing make revisions to edit.
- Write a version of the classic five subdivisions of a text literary composition. Answer the query in the first subdivisions of a text of your literary composition. State and support one cogent evidence for your respond in each of the following paragraphs. Answer the query in dissimilar words in your concluding subdivisions of a text.

Preparing for an Essay Exam

- Get a sense for the type of literary composition examination the prof generally gives e. g. having little length vs. lengthy cerebration questions.

- Try to acquire some thought of the general field that shall be covered i. e. concepts issues theories etcetera.
- Carefully inspection teaching notes to ascertain which broad areas have constituted middle discussion subjects.
- Carefully inspection writings s. Link and or supplement enormous areas here with those in your notes.
- Mentally test yourself What enormous concepts and relationships were covered Now what individual features support these
- Be capable to communicate or express by writing a concise linear boundary that cover the matter.
- Remember Present a auditory event generalization then establish it with appropriate detail.
- Be well known with the terminology being used in the track. Be capable to comprehend concepts and use appropriate conditions.

Taking the Exam

- Listen for any of or involving the mouth directions if any.
- Read the questions carefully. What are they asking
- Be sure you comprehend the query. What is the controlling thought What are the prime words Underline them.
- How is the respond to be given Is the query asking for fact Opinion Explanation Comparison
- If the query seems equivocal
- a. Seek clarification from the prof
- b. if nevertheless not well defined state of matter your interpretation of the query before attempting to respond it. Remember literary composition questions are aimed at concepts and the accent in the track so you must be capable to conceptualize succinctly respond and support your generalization with sufficient individual features.
- Define any undefined conditions for instance some conditions may have equivocal implications if not clearly defined.
- Think via your respond. Then move reverse and reread the query to make sure that you are answering what is asked.

Writing the Answers

- Remember to get time to consider make notes and prepare a unsmooth linear boundary before you cause to start to communicate or express by writing the literary composition
- a. Develop the brief statement assertion.

- b. Support the assertion with individual features.
- Once you have your brief statement in linear boundary form spread extend in one or more spread upon it and communicate or express by writing it in written form tactfully and clearly.
- Budget your time so that you are not forced to rushing via your final examination literary composition because you expend too much time on the earlier one s.
- Allow a little time to proofread for grammar spelling mistakes omissions etcetera.

Multiple Choice examination tips

General Rule Break each query into the stem and the alternatives. Get an know-how of the stem before looking at and choosing an alternative. Underline prime conditions and hint words in the stem. When you be operating or functioning into undefined terminology give a definition for in your own words. Think of the correct respond and then see for it among the alternatives.

1. Don't make a guess too soon You must select not only a correct respond but the best respond. It is therefore significant that you interpret something all of the options and not stop when you come upon one that seems plausible.

2. You must select not only a technically correct respond but the most completely correct respond. Since all of the above and none of the above are very inclusive statements these options when being used tend to be correct more frequently than would be predicted by hazard alone.

3. Be wary of options which comprise unqualified absolutes such as never always is are guarantees ensures. Such statements are highly restrictive and very hard to protect. They are rarely though they may sometimes be correct options.

4. The less frequently stated converse of the above is that carefully meeting the standards and requirements resistant to change or guarded statements tend to be correct more frequently than would be predicted by hazard alone. Other things being same kind gracious act options containing such qualifying phrases as may sometimes be or can occasionally outcome in.

5. Be wary of the extra lengthy or jargony possibility. These are frequently being used as decoys.

6. Use your information of ordinary prefixes suffixes and speech roots to make intelligent guesses about terminology that you don't see. A information of the prefix hyper for instance would hint you that hypertension refers to high not being at small elevation blood insistency.

7. Be alert to bestow aways in grammatical construction. The correct respond to an individual instance stem which ends in an would obviously be an possibility starting with a vowel. Watch also for agreement of subjects and verbs.

8. Utilize intelligence and insights that you've acquired in working via the complete test to move reverse and respond earlier items that you weren't sure of.

9. If you are not sure of an respond make a guess. . but do so methodically. Eliminate some choices you see are incorrect then tie each alternative reverse to the stem of the query to view if it fits. Narrow down the alternative to one or two alternatives and then liken them and name how they vary. Finally make an informed make a guess.

10. If you have absolutely no thought what the respond is can't use any of the above techniques and there is no scoring punishment for guessing select possibility B or C. Studies indicate that these are correct slightly more frequently than would be predicted by hazard alone.

11. When you acquire all the above none of the above or a b not c type questions care provide treatment treat medically each alternative as a real dit query and tie it reverse to the query stem.

12. Think the respond is based on error Maybe you should change it Studies indicate that when students change their answers they usually change them to the based on error respond. Therefore if you were fairly sure you were correct the first time get out the respond as it is.

13. Finally the best manner to make sure choice of the correct possibility is to see the correct respond. A speech to the test wise is sufficient.

Test Taking Strategies

Test Taking Study Tips

From my personal practice I've learned that test taking can be easier with a some easy tips. First always research in a quiescent environment that is well lit. Studying should cause to start at least ten days in advance. Give yourself manageable sections to research each day. This manner it shall not be overwhelming. Know ahead of time exactly what to research for. The professors frequently bestow ideas as to what the test shall be like. Take gain of this. Quiz yourself on the matter you studied without using your books or notes. Doing this shall bestow you an thought of how you shall do on the test. Allow yourself a fifteen to twenty unit of time equal to 60 seconds destroy for every 60 period of time of studying. During this time loosen unwind with a use one's feet to advance or a talk with a acquaintance. Before the examination take in solid food properly and have plenty of catch one's take a breather. Following these tips shall support you when it comes to test time.

Organization Ideas

First of all I commend that you acquire a good night's slumber. Get up with time to give part with. Shower shampoo have a good morning meal or midday meal. Go to the test early. Be confident about it. Second I'd tell that when you're studying bring order and organization to matter for more result driven memorizing. Usually professors have organized matter such things as seven elements eight causes six results. Always use their organization. If they have not achieved this then you must impose your own organization. It is easier to recall four headings with eight elements under each than to recall thirty sole elements. So even if your headings have to be unnatural only use anything that's going to support you recall all the matter. And terminal do not over research. Whenever students pull blanks during an examination its because they have over studied. Study only lengthy enough to be capable to replicate to yourself once most of the matter. Then move on to something else. Perhaps later return to the previous matter to view if you have nevertheless retained it.

Last Minute Preparation

If you've dug an academic opening into or through something for yourself don't overwhelming fear. Although little except prayers and luck can support students who never move to grade or fissure a volume all semester there's one helpful proficiency for students who have fallen behind at mid conditions and finals. CRAM. First select carefully the most significant subjects from your matter. Don't adjudicate to lightly see everything. Spend 25 percentage of your time cramming and 75 drilling yourself. The prime to cramming is memorization. Recite. Repeat. Then loosen unwind. Although cramming can't substitute for a defective or inadequate one learning it's business table generative to scold yourself for not studying more effectively. Learn from your error. Think of cramming only as the lifeboat that bailed out a sinking ship.

Memory Tips and Test Taking Strategies

Knowing More Remembering it Longer

Remembering Strategies

- Select
- Select what you need to recall.
- Ask the instructor
- Examine your grade notes
- Read the writings assignments
- Study the handouts
- Remember
- Choose your techniques that shall support you recall.
- Visualize
- Associate
- Apply
- Repeat
- Use mnemonic devices
- Review Read Recite Rewrite

Use these techniques to hold onto what you need to recall in your memory.

Using Mnemonic Devices to Remember Information

- Rhyme. A rhyme is a verse form or verse that uses words that end with the same auditory event. Example Thirty days has September April June and November. All the catch one's take a breather have thirty one except February which has twenty eight.

- Acronym. An acronym is a speech that can be pronounced that is made by using the first written message addressed of another words. Example The names of the five Great Lakes in the U. S. form the acronym HOMES Huron Ontario Michigan Erie Superior.
- Abbreviation. An abridgement is a group of letters made from the first written message addressed of each speech to be remembered. Example FBI is an abridgement for the Federal Bureau of Investigation.
- Acrostic. An acrostic conviction or phrase is formed by words start with the first written message addressed of each speech to be remembered. Example The phrase very vigorous feline might be being used to recall the three typed of blood vessels in the human body veins arteries capillaries.
- Pegwords. A pegword is a speech that helps you recall something by forming a visual representation in your mind. Pegwords are being used to recall lists of things. Each pegword helps you recall one thing. If you memorize 10 pegwords then you can use them to recall 10 things. If you memorize 20 pegwords you can recall 20 things.
- Using Repetition to Remember Information

You have probably being used repeat many times without realizing it. Anytime you have interpret something said or written something a numeral of times to recall it you have being used repeat. A good manner to recall intelligence when using repeat is to interpret something tell and communicate or express by writing what you need to recall. For instance if you need to recall a register of words and their definitions here is how to use repeat to do this

- Read aloud the speech and its determination. If you need to use a lexicon to support you pronounce a speech.
- With your eyes unopen tell the speech and its determination.
- Without looking at the speech communicate or express by writing the speech and its determination.
- Repeat the steps until you can communicate or express by writing the speech and its determination from memory three times without an faulty.
- Do this for each speech on the register.

Four Ways to Forget

- Disuse. Information not periodically being used withers and disappears. Do you recall all of your previous telephone set numbers
- Interference. It is simple to confound materials that are like and connected. When confused we are more plausible to blank draw a fail to remember which is which. Learning two like foreign languages at the same time may being here some problems.
- Repression. We have very unattackable systems of cognitive content held as TRUE. Sometimes what we memorize does not fit with what we believe. When in incompatibility of dates or events odds are our beliefs shall win. Believing that we are no good at remembering names shall make it all that much more hard to memorize fresh names.
- Not learning it in the first place. This is probably the numeral one culprit in forgetting. Even if we've been exposed to something unless we solidify the learning we are not plausible to recall it.

More Test Taking Strategies

Taking Objective Tests

If you are taking an nonsubjective test several alternative real dit or comparable type you shall probably gain with effort your best results by following this procedure

Read an individual instance via quickly with high immersion and respond on the base of your first impression.

Then re interpret something the individual instance asking yourself what it really means and expressing its cerebration in your own words.

Ask yourself if your first respond nevertheless appears correct in emitting light of your close test of the individual instance but do not change your respond because of a mere consider unlikely.

Always hold onto in mind that your instructor is not attempting to fast one you in the questions. They are designed to gauge your information of a theme not your ingenuity in solving verbal puzzles. So don't out bright yourself looking for devious tricky interpretations and ignoring the obvious straightforward signification.

Essay Tests

In taking a test where you are to communicate or express by writing answers in your own words observe these guidelines

Read the query carefully. Then re interpret something it and without unnecessary stops its signification in your own words. Check each speech in the query to be sure that your interpretation omitted nothing significant. To bestow a satisfactory respond to a query you have to correctly comprehend what the query is asking.

Answer the questions you see first. This manner you shall be sure not to use all your time puzzling over questions you do not see the answers to and then be operating or functioning having little length of time for writing answers you see well.

Outline your respond on a part of scrape material for writing or printing on before starting to communicate or express by writing it in complete. In this manner you can bring order and organization to your thoughts and control your respond against the query for possible omissions. Writing from your linear boundary you can being here what you see more clearly and completely than you could if you only started writing down your thoughts as they came to you.

Write with a good writing implement or a well sharpened No. 2 writing implement so that your writing can be easily interpret something. Also timepiece your penmanship spelling and punctuation.

Read over your answers after you have ruined your material for writing or printing on checking for cerebration and completeness as well as for spelling punctuation and conviction structure. All these factors are connected to your mastery of track matter. What is involved in answering a query completely is determined by the question's choice of words and the preferences of personal professors. From the numeral of questions on the test and the amount of time you are allotted you can form a unsmooth approximation of how fully you should respond the questions.

number your questions and answers before you hand your material for writing or printing on in to be sure you did not fail to notice anything. Be sure your pages are in correct order so the instructor shall not have to shuffle via them trying to sort them out.

Preparing for Finals

At least a calendar week before exams work shift into overdrive by start an extensive inspection. Set up a detailed time schedule for the remainder of the semester.

Attend all classes as instructors frequently use the terminal some classes earlier to an examination to summarize inspection and clear make comprehensible.

Prepare brief statement sheets one set for writings and one for teaching.

Pick out the most significant facts.

Organize intelligence into categories in a way dissimilar from the manner you first leaned it. For instance History is chronological so adjudicate organizing your notes under headings that emphasize time instead of themes.

Review brief statement sheets and comprise prime words for significant facts.

Recite intelligence orally ACTIVE learning is fundamental How you store intelligence determines how well you retrieve it so use all your senses when reviewing.

If you must cram hold up against trying to memorize too much matter. Select only a handful of facts even at the hazard of leaving out something significant.

During Exams

Arrive early and recall to BREATHE

Read and hear to directions.

Skim the examination and design your time.

Answer the simple questions first to make feeling of trust and make force. You may work the test from reverse to atmospheric phenomenon at the boundary between two air masses answering the terminal query first.

A query you can't respond can be skipped frequently another query shall trigger your memory or supply that elusive respond.

Answer all questions.

Save a some minutes at the end to move reverse over questions you skipped to inspection your answers and see for careless mistakes.

Stress Management Test Anxiety

The ABC's of Eliminating Exam Anxiety

Think Positively. Thoughts such as I haven't studied enough and I don't see the matter shall only augment your anxiousness level. Instead adjudicate to fell good about what you do see. You perceive sound it all the time but a confirming mental attitude goes a lengthy manner.

Take a having great spatial extension downward breath. It really shall support you calm quieten down. Think of a money for helping to find criminals that you'll bestow yourself when you're via maybe midday meal out or a film with a acquaintance.

If you pull a not filled in don't overwhelming fear. It happens all the time. Take a some minutes to sit be seated reverse and stay in one place and anticipate something for it to come reverse to you.

Don't see around to view what your classmates are doing. If you're having doubts about how well you're doing and you view someone who looks like they're aceing the examination it shall only total to your anxiousness.

Prepare well for your exams. People who see the matter rarely acquire neural. Review regularly and bestow yourself practice tests.

Keep things in perspective. Although exams are significant they're not a substance of life or departure from life. In later years nobody shall inquire you what grades you received on your exams. They fail to win significance over time.

Stress Management

Here are a some qualities that shall support you invent your institution of higher education endurance skills.

Be resilient. It's easier to deal with life if you can adapt to any state of affairs. For instance if you can be hardworking and dedicated at examination time yet be capable to get out it all behind when exams are over you'll be better capable to handle whatever you human face.

Be not given to gentleness or sentimentality. You have to be capable to see after yourself. People may be the source of pain you or scuttlebutt about you but it's significant to hold onto their actions from affecting you.

Before you react though be sure you are interpreting others conduct correctly. What you may sense as a hurtful act may not have been intended as such. Stress can make you powerful stroke things out of dimension.

Keep laughing. A good manner to hold onto a confirming mindset is to book on to your sense of sense of humor. Don't get things too seriously and you'll be better capable to hold onto things in perspective.

Be open minded. It's simple to be tending to find errors and flaws of a state of affairs or prof particularly if those around you are doing so. Don't let others be a disconfirming effect of one thing or person on you. Keep an open mind come to your own conclusions and you'll enjoy love to do things more fully.

Meet fresh people. One of the best therapies for depressive clinical depression is to move out and assemble fresh people or take part in a fresh trait of being active. You may discover that despite you difficulties there's nevertheless a great deal out there to enjoy love to do.

Don't perspiration the small fill tightly. A renowned cardiologist's investigation of ethics for dealing with tenseness 1 Don't perspiration the small fill tightly. 2 It's all small fill tightly.

Use the Five Year Rule. Ask yourself Five years from presently how impatient shall this problem be Nine times out of ten the respond is Not very significant. The five yr direction can hold onto you from blowing the state of affairs out of dimension.

7 Ways to Cope With it All

Talk to someone. Don't vessel your problems up. Go to someone you trustful relationship and acquire it off your chest of dresser. Sometimes only verbalizing the problem can support you to view it in a dissimilar emitting light.

Make your get break run away from confinement. Taking a destroy from a hard state of affairs can do wonders for your enclose in a frame of mind.

Let it out. Release your frustration in a generative manner a tough amusement or pastime of racquetball for instance shall ease your tautness

Forget about it. Sometimes you've only got to tell This isn't significant enough to bestow my time to and shift on from whatever's got you down.

Do something nice. If you discover yourself thinking about your own worries too much focus on someone else who's dealing with a not given to gentleness or sentimentality state of affairs. You'll acquire a good touch sensation from doing something nice for them and you'll blank draw a fail to remember about your own troubles.

Do one thing at a time. If your workload seems overwhelming don't acquire discouraged. Take the most significant task that's haunting you and begin in on it. Accomplishing even one of your to do's can make you undergo an emotional sensation like you're reverse in discipline in personal activities.

Give yourself a destroy. Some people make tenseness by setting standards that are too high to extend touch. Don't adjudicate to be best sometimes you'll have to be slaked with good enough.

Even More Test Taking Strategies

1. Before you begin discover out if there is a punishment for guessing and if you can select more than one respond.

2. Read the questions and all possible answers carefully.

3. Be particularly careful about questions with the choices all of the above and none of the above.

4. Underline prime words and qualifiers such as never always and so on.

5. Answer all of the questions you see first.

6. Make a indication of damage next to those you can't respond so you can move reverse to them later.

7. After you having every necessary part the questions you see move reverse and reread the ones you didn't respond the first time.

8. If you nevertheless can't respond a query the second time via interpret something the query then stop and adjudicate to consider of an respond. Look to view if one of the choices is like to your respond.

9. Start by eliminating those answers that you see are not correct and then select among the alternatives.

10. Read via all of the answers very carefully and then move reverse to the query. Sometimes you can select carefully up clues only by thinking about the dissimilar answers you have been given to select from.

11. Try paraphrasing the query and then recalling some examples.

12. Read the query separately with each alternative several alternative respond.

Specific Hints for Answering Multiple alternative Questions

1. Remember that a best respond to every query may not be provided you must select the best respond obtainable.

2. Cross out answers you see are incorrect. Eliminating answers is helpful because it focuses your faculty or power of mental concentration on the most sensible options. If you consider all options are incorrect the correct respond is none of the above.

3. Be sure to interpret something all the possible answers to a query particularly when the first respond is correct. Remember that the another options could also be correct. In this case all of the above would be the correct reaction.

4. Try not to see at the answers when you return to hard items. Instead interpret something the query amount of something available for use your own respond and then see for the possibility that is closest to your reaction.

5. Use the following clues which may signal correct answers only when you have no thought of the respond and must make a guess

a. The longest respond is frequently correct

b. The most having every necessary part and inconclusive respond is frequently correct

c. An respond in the intermediate part or section particularly one with the most words is frequently correct

d. If two answers have the contrary signification one of them is probably correct

e. Answers with qualifiers such as generally probably most frequently some sometimes and usually are frequently correct

f. Answers with perfect or complete words such as all always everyone everybody never no one nobody and only are usually incorrect

Taking Tests

Before the Test

Review notes daily

Join a research group

Read the textbook

Ask you instructor or the research group questions

Study consistently but get research breaks

Try to make a guess what questions the instructor shall inquire

Write your own test before the actual test

Make flashcards

During the test

RELAX

Read the directions until you are sure you comprehend

Scan the test

Plan your time

Make sure you are well defined on what is being asked

Ask questions if you do not comprehend

For literary composition questions make an linear boundary of your answers

Make sure you have put an respond for every query never get out a not filled in

Write clearly

Check your test before handing it in if you have time

Do not change answers unless you are sure of the fresh respond

After the test

Look up any answers you were unsure about

Go over test and correct any mistakes

Ask the prof if you are nevertheless unclear on an respond

Begin preparing for the next test

Ask yourself how you could have improved your test preparedness

Exam time Hints for result driven studying

The examination time is a time when tenseness levels are higher than usual. Stress can be confirming helping you to stick stay put motivated and focused. However too much tenseness can be unhelpful it can make you undergo an emotional sensation overwhelmed confused exhausted and edgy.

It's significant to adjudicate and hold onto things in perspective and discover ways of reducing tenseness if things appear to be getting on top upper upside of you. This factsheet gives you some suggestions of things you can do to maximise your research time and support you memorize better. Check out Exam time Hints for managing tenseness for more tips on managing examination tenseness.

Study habits

Study field Having a good research field can make a vast difference of conflict to how well you memorize. Study in a well lit quiescent field away from noises and people in the house. If this is impossible it might be better to research at the library. Make sure your desk is clean and organised it means you can focus one's attention on studying and learning not trying to discover intelligence.

Find out about the examination Find out what data data formatting the examination shall get i. e. Are the questions in literary composition having little length respond or several alternative data data formatting Is the examination open volume or unopen volume Knowing how the examination is marked and what dimension of your entire indication of damage it's value might also be helpful.

To do lists Make a to do register before each research meeting. Breaking tasks down into small managable tasks shall make it less overwhelming. Cross them off as you move.

Past examination papers Ask your instructor for earlier than the present time examination papers. They can be a utile understanding into what your examination shall be like and can also supply a guidebook for what you see and the areas in which you need support. If possible practice some under examination conditions and acquire your instructor to indication of damage them.

Study groups Forming a studying group can be a helpful manner to make revisions to your notes and work via earlier than the present time examination questions it can also support you undergo an emotional sensation supported hold onto you motivated and focused. If you have questions about your work a research group may be a good place to have them answered. Ask your instructor if they see of anyone else interested in studying with another people.

Switch the phone or email off If you discover that you are being distracted by the phone or emails it might support to put the answering machine on or acquire others in the house to get messages for a while. You can always boxing ring people reverse later.

Wallpaper Write down prime concepts you have to memorize on small sheets of material for writing or printing on followed by examples of how they are being used. Post these sheets around your house Eg your piece of furniture on the toilet swinging or sliding barrier in atmospheric phenomenon at the boundary between two air masses of the CD assemblage. It helps with remembering things like equations quotes and foreign languages.

Ask lots of questions of your teachers or tutor Your instructor or tutor can support if you are having worry developing a research modus operandi or need support with know-how subjects or a specific topic. Asking for support does not stand for you're a failing or stupid it's bright to telephone tap into their practice and information to support you give a performance better. Keep going reverse to them if you're nevertheless unsure or you have more questions. It's their job to be obtainable for you.

Know your preferred learning editorial directions Some people work better using writings based memory tools like acronyms Eg ROYGBIV colours of the colored light in the sky acrostics Eg Every Good Boy Deserves Fruit. Other people discover more optical tools more utile Eg mind maps or tree diagrams.

Take steady breaks Getting up arousing deep emotion around and away from your desk at least every 50 minutes for 10 minutes makes you focus one's attention and memorize better.

Revise and memorize don't only re interpret something Sometimes reading via notes does not outcome in learning or know-how. Include the following in revising each topic

vocabulary technical conditions definitions

summaries of points

formulae rules diagrams charts

way to comprehend relationships.

Time management

Avoid procrastination Procrastination is when you do everything else but the task you need to do. It is standard to procrastinate a little. However too much procrastination can only total to your tenseness and can outcome in you not giving yourself enough time to prepare. Managing your time and setting realistic goals for each research meeting can be helpful ways to evade procrastinating and make tasks appear less overwhelming.

Make a research arrival and departure schedule Write down all the things you need to do each day of the calendar week and how lengthy you need for each including time for enough slumber absence of tension and physical exercise. Find out the day of the month of each examination and work out a research arrival and departure schedule principal up to them. Include tests that shall support you name gaps in your information. This can bestow you some counsel and support you focus on what to research each calendar week or day.

Use your frees Studying in the educational institution library during your frees gives you admittance to lots of intelligence obtainable on the quotation shelves. Some matter such as small part representative of the whole solutions frequently can't be taken out of the library or can be too lengthy to run off.

More Information

Most libraries or bookshop stock a gamma of books on result driven studying and time management that can support trim examination tenseness.

FINDING AND APPLYING FOR CCNP Routing and Switching JOBS AND EVALUATING OFFERS

Finding—and getting—a job you want can be a challenging process, but knowing more about job search methods and application techniques can increase your chances of success. And knowing how to judge the job offers you receive makes it more likely that you will end up with the best possible job.

- Where to learn About Job Openings
- Job Search Methods
- Applying for a Job
- Job Interview Tips
- Evaluating a Job Offer

Where to Learn About Job Openings

- Personal contacts
- School career planning and placement offices
- Employers
- Classified ads:
    1. National and local newspapers
    2. Professional journals
    3. Trade magazines
    4. Internet resources
- Professional associations
- Labor unions
- State employment service offices
- Federal Government
- Community agencies
- Private employment agencies and career consultants
- Internships

Job Search Methods

Finding a job can take months of time and effort. But you can speed the process by using many methods to find job openings. Data from the Bureau of Labor Statistics suggest that people who use many job search methods find jobs faster than people who use only one or two.

Personal contacts.

Many jobs are never advertised. People get them by talking to friends, family, neighbors, acquaintances, teachers, former coworkers, and others who know of an opening. Be sure to tell people that you are looking for a job because the people you know may be some of the most effective resources for your search. To develop new contacts, join student, community, or professional organizations.

School career planning and placement offices.

High school and college placement offices help their students and alumni find jobs. Some invite recruiters to use their facilities for interviews or career fairs. They also may have lists of open jobs. Most also offer career counseling, career testing, and job search advice. Some have career resource libraries; host workshops on job search strategy, resume writing, letter writing, and effective interviewing; critique drafts of resumes; conduct mock interviews; and sponsor job fairs.

Employers.

Directly contacting employers is one of the most successful means of job hunting. Through library and Internet research, develop a list of potential employers in your desired career field. Then call these employers and check their Web sites for job openings. Web sites and business directories can tell you how to apply for a position or whom to contact. Even if no open positions are posted, do not hesitate to contact the employer: You never know when a job might become available.

Consider asking for an informational interview with people working in the career you want to learn more. Ask them how they got started, what they like and dislike about the work, what type of qualifications are necessary for the job, and what type of personality succeeds in that position. In addition to giving you career information, they may be able to put you in contact with other people who might hire you, and they can keep you in mind if a position opens up.

Classified ads.

The "Help Wanted" ads in newspapers and the Internet list numerous jobs, and many people find work by responding to these ads. But when using classified ads, keep the following in mind:

- Follow all leads to find a job; do not rely solely on the classifieds.
- Answer ads promptly, because openings may be filled quickly, even before the ad stops appearing in the paper.
- Read the ads every day, particularly the Sunday edition, which usually includes the most listings.
- Keep a record of all ads to which you have responded, including the specific skills, educational background, and personal qualifications required for the position.

Internet resources.

The Internet includes many job hunting Web sites with job listings. Some job boards provide National listings of all kinds; others are local. Some relate to a specific type of work; others are general. To find good prospects, begin with an Internet search using keywords related to the job you want. Also look for the sites of related professional associations.

Also consider checking Internet forums, also called message boards. These are online discussion groups where anyone may post and read messages. Use forums specific to your profession or to career-related topics to post questions or messages and to read about the job searches or career experiences of other people.

In online job databases, remember that job listings may be posted by field or discipline, so begin your search using keywords. Many Web sites allow job seekers to post their resumes online for free.

Professional associations. Many professions have associations that offer employment information, including career planning, educational programs, job listings, and job placement. To use these services, associations usually require that you be a member; information can be obtained directly from an association through the Internet, by telephone, or by mail.

Labor unions.

Labor unions provide various employment services to members and potential members, including apprenticeship programs that teach a specific trade or skill. Contact the appropriate labor union or State apprenticeship council for more information.

State employment service offices.

The State employment service, sometimes called the Job Service, operates in coordination with the U.S. Department of Labor's Employment and Training Administration. Local offices, found nationwide, help job seekers to find jobs and help employers to find qualified workers at no cost to either. To find the office nearest you, look in the State government telephone listings under "Job Service" or "Employment."

Job matching and referral.

At the State employment service office, an interviewer will determine if you are "job ready" or if you need help from counseling and testing services to assess your occupational aptitudes and interests and to help you choose and prepare for a career. After you are job ready, you may examine available job listings and select openings that interest you. A staff member can then describe the job openings in detail and arrange for interviews with prospective employers.

Services for special groups.

By law, veterans are entitled to priority job placement at State employment service centers. If you are a veteran, a veterans' employment representative can inform you of available assistance and help you to deal with problems.

State employment service offices also refer people to opportunities available under the Workforce Investment Act (WIA) of 1998. Educational and career services and referrals are provided to employers and job seekers, including adults, dislocated workers, and youth. These programs help to prepare people to participate in the State's workforce, increase their employment and earnings potential, improve their educational and occupational skills, and reduce their dependency on welfare.

Federal Government.

Information on obtaining a position with the Federal Government is available from the U.S. Office of Personnel Management (OPM) through USAJOBS, the Federal Government's official employment information system. This resource for locating and applying for job opportunities can be accessed through the Internet at http://www.usajobs.opm.gov or through an interactive voice response telephone system at (703) 724-1850 or TDD (978) 461-8404. These numbers are not toll free, and charges may result.

Community agencies.

Many nonprofit organizations, including religious institutions and vocational rehabilitation agencies, offer counseling, career development, and job placement services, generally targeted to a particular group, such as women, youths, minorities, ex-offenders, or older workers.

Private employment agencies and career consultants.

Private agencies can save you time and they will contact employers who otherwise might be difficult to locate. But these agencies may charge for their services. Most operate on a commission basis, charging a percentage of the first-year salary paid to a successful applicant. You or the hiring company will pay the fee. Find out the exact cost and who is responsible for paying associated fees before using the service. When determining if the service is worth the cost, consider any guarantees that the agency offers.

Internships.

Many people find jobs with business and organizations with whom they have interned or volunteered. Look for internships and volunteer opportunities on job boards, career centers, and company and association Web sites, but also check community service organizations and volunteer opportunity databases. Some internships and long-term volunteer positions come with stipends and all provide experience and the chance to meet employers and other good networking contacts.

APPLYING FOR A CCNP ROUTING AND SWITCHING JOB

After you have found some jobs that interest you, the next step is to apply for them. You will almost always need to complete resumes or application forms and cover letters. Later, you will probably need to go on interviews to meet with employers face to face.

Resumes and application forms.

Resumes and application forms give employers written evidence of your qualifications and skills. The goal of these documents is to prove—as clearly and directly as possible—how your qualifications match the job's requirements. Do this by highlighting the experience, accomplishments, education, and skills that most closely fit the job you want.

Gathering information.

Resumes and application forms both include the same information. As a first step, gather the following facts:

- Contact information, including your name, mailing address, e-mail address (if you have one you check often), and telephone number.
- Type of work or specific job you are seeking or a qualifications summary, which describes your best skills and experience in just a few lines.
- Education, including school name and its city and State, months and years of attendance, highest grade completed or diploma or degree awarded, and major subject or subjects studied. Also consider listing courses and awards that might be relevant to the position. Include a grade point average if you think it would help in getting the job.
- Experience, paid and volunteer. For each job, include the job title, name and location of employer, and dates of employment. Briefly describe your job duties and major accomplishments. In a resume, use phrases instead of sentences to describe your work; write, for example, "Supervised 10 children" instead of writing "I supervised 10 children."
- Special skills. You might list computer skills, proficiency in foreign

languages, achievements, or and membership in organizations in a separate section.
- References. Be ready to provide references if requested. Good references could be former employers, coworkers, or teachers or anyone else who can describe your abilities and job-related traits. You will be asked to provide contact information for the people you choose.

Throughout the application or resume, focus on accomplishments that relate most closely to the job you want. You can even use the job announcement as a guide, using some of the same words and phrases to describe your work and education.

Look for concrete examples that show your skills. When describing your work experience, for instance, you might say that you increased sales by 10 percent, finished a task in half the usual time, or received three letters of appreciation from customers.

Choosing a format.

After gathering the information you want to present, the next step is to put it in the proper format. In an application form, the format is set. Just fill in the blanks. But make sure you fill it out completely and follow all instructions. Do not omit any requested information. Consider making a copy of the form before filling it out, in case you make a mistake and have to start over. If possible, have someone else look over the form before submitting it.

In a resume, there are many ways of organizing the information you want to include, but the most important information should usually come first. Most applicants list their past jobs in reverse chronological order, describing their most recent employment first and working backward. But some applicants use a functional format, organizing their work experience under headings that describe their major skills. They then include a brief work history section that lists only job titles, employers, and dates of employment. Still other applicants choose a format that combines these two approaches in some way. Choose the style that best showcases your skills and experience.

Whatever format you choose, keep your resume short. Many experts recommend that new workers use a one-page resume. Avoid long blocks of text and italicized material. Consider using bullets to highlight duties or key accomplishments.

Before submitting your resume, make sure that it is easy to read. Are the headings clear and consistently formatted with bold or some other style of type? Is the type face large enough? Then, ask at least two people to proofread the resume for spelling and other errors and make sure you use your computer's spell checker.

Keep in mind that many employers scan resumes into databases, which they then search for specific keywords or phrases. The keywords are usually nouns referring to experience, education, personal characteristics, or industry buzz words. Identify keywords by reading tasks and qualifications in the job ad; use these same words in your resume. For example, if the role includes customer service tasks, use the words "customer service" on your resume. Scanners sometimes misread paper resumes, which could mean some of your keywords don't get into the database. So, if you know that your resume will be scanned, and you have the option, e-mail an electronic version. If you must submit a paper resume, make it scannable by using a simple font and avoiding underlines, italics, and graphics. It is also a good idea to send a traditionally formatted resume along with your scannable resume, with a note on each marking its purpose.

Resume and KSA (knowledge, skills & abilities) tips:

Pay Attention to Keywords

Whether you're writing your first resume, updating an existing one, or answering a position's Knowledges, Skills, and Abilities (KSA's), stop and think about which keywords you need to add. You could be the most qualified person for the position, but you could be lost in a sea of applicants without the right keywords.

A Single Keyword Communicates Multiple Skills and Qualifications

When a recruiter reads the keyword "analyst," he or she might assume you have experience in collecting data, evaluating effectiveness, and researching and developing new processes. Just one keyword can have tremendous power and deliver a huge message.

Study Job Announcements

This is the best way to determine important keywords. Review several job announcements and their questions for your ideal position. The jobs don't have to be in your geographic target area. The idea is to find skills, experience, education and other credentials important in your field. You will probably find keywords frequently mentioned by different agencies. Focus on the "requirements," "skills" or "qualifications" sections of job ads, and look for "buzzwords" and desirable credentials for your ideal job.

Be Concise

Don't confuse telling your story with creating your autobiography. Recruiters are inundated with applications and are faced with weeding out the good from the bad. The first step involves quickly skimming through submissions and eliminating candidates who clearly are not qualified. Therefore, your application needs to pass the skim test. Look at your resume and/or KSA's and ask yourself:

- Can a hiring manager see my main credentials within 10 to 15 seconds?
- Does critical information jump off the page?
- Do I effectively sell myself on the top quarter of the first page?

The Sales Pitch

Because applications are quickly skimmed during the first pass, it is crucial your resume and KSA's get right to work selling your credentials. Your key selling points need to be prominently displayed at the top of the first page of the resume and directly address each question asked in the KSA section. For example, if an advanced degree is an important qualification, it shouldn't be buried at the end of a four-page resume. If a KSA question asks about your writing ability, immediately detail your experience instead of enjoyment of it.

Use an Editor's Eye

Many workers are proud of their careers and feel the information on a resume should reflect everything they've accomplished. However, a resume shouldn't contain every detail and KSA's should only address the question at hand. So be judicious. If your college days are far behind you, does it really matter that you pledged a fraternity or delivered pizza? The editing step will be difficult if you are holding on to your past for emotional reasons.

Use Numbers to Highlight Your Accomplishments

If you were a recruiter looking at a resume or an answer to a KSA, which of the following entries would impress you more:

- Wrote news releases.
- Wrote 25 news releases in a three-week period under daily deadlines.

Clearly the second statement carries more weight. Why? Because it uses numbers to quantify the writer's accomplishment, giving it a context that helps the interviewer understand the degree of difficulty involved in the task. Numbers are powerful resume tools that will help your accomplishments draw the attention they deserve from prospective employers. With just a little thought, you can find effective ways to quantify your successes on your resume.

Think Money

For-profit, nonprofit, and government organizations alike are and always will be concerned about money. So as you contemplate your accomplishments and prepare to present them on your resume or in your KSA's, think about ways you've saved money, earned money, or managed money in your internships, part-time jobs and extracurricular activities so far. A few possibilities that might appear on a typical college student's resume:

- Identified, researched and recommended a new Internet Service Provider, cutting the company's online costs by 15 percent.
- Wrote prospect letter that has brought in more than $25,000 in donations to date.
- Managed a student organization budget of more than $7,000.

Think Time

You've heard the old saying, "Time is money," and it's true. Companies and organizations are constantly looking for ways to save time and do things more efficiently. They're also necessarily concerned about meeting deadlines, both internal and external. So whatever you can do on your resume or in your KSA's to show that you can save time, make time or manage time will grab your reader's immediate attention. Here are some time-oriented entries that might appear on a typical college student's resume:

- Assisted with twice-monthly payroll activities, ensuring employees were paid as expected and on time.
- Attended high school basketball games, interviewed players and coaches afterward, and composed 750-word articles by an 11 p.m. deadline.
- Suggested procedures that decreased average order-processing time from 10 minutes to five minutes.

Cover letters.

When sending a resume, most people include a cover letter to introduce themselves to the prospective employer. Most cover letters are no more than three short paragraphs. Your cover letter should capture the employer's attention, follow a business letter format, and usually should include the following information:

- Name and address of the specific person to whom the letter is addressed.
- Reason for your interest in the company or position.
- Your main qualifications for the position.
- Request for an interview.
- Your home and work telephone numbers.

If you send a scannable resume, you should also include a scannable cover letter, which avoids graphics, fancy fonts, italics, and underlines.

As with your resume, it may be helpful to look for examples on the Internet or in books at your local library or bookstore, but be sure not to copy letters directly from other sources.

CCNP ROUTING AND SWITCHING JOB INTERVIEW TIPS

An interview gives you the opportunity to showcase your qualifications to an employer, so it pays to be well prepared. The following information provides some helpful hints.

Preparation:

- Learn about the organization.
- Have a specific job or jobs in mind.
- Review your qualifications for the job.
- Be ready to briefly describe your experience, showing how it relates it the job.
- Be ready to answer broad questions, such as "Why should I hire you?" "Why do you want this job?" "What are your strengths and weaknesses?"
- Practice an interview with a friend or relative.

Personal appearance:

- Be well groomed.
- Dress appropriately.
- Do not chew gum or smoke.

The interview:

- Be early.
- Learn the name of your interviewer and greet him or her with a firm handshake.
- Use good manners with everyone you meet.
- Relax and answer each question concisely.
- Use proper English—avoid slang.
- Be cooperative and enthusiastic.
- Use body language to show interest—use eye contact and don't slouch.
- Ask questions about the position and the organization, but avoid questions whose answers can easily be found on the company Web site.
- Also avoid asking questions about salary and benefits unless a job offer is made.
- Thank the interviewer when you leave and shake hands.

- Send a short thank you note.

Information to bring to an interview:

- Social Security card.
- Government-issued identification (driver's license).
- Resume or application. Although not all employers require a resume, you should be able to furnish the interviewer information about your education, training, and previous employment.
- References. Employers typically require three references. Get permission before using anyone as a reference. Make sure that they will give you a good reference. Try to avoid using relatives as references.
- Transcripts. Employers may require an official copy of transcripts to verify grades, coursework, dates of attendance, and highest grade completed or degree awarded.

EVALUATING A CCNP ROUTING AND SWITCHING JOB OFFER

Once you receive a job offer, you must decide if you want the job. Fortunately, most organizations will give you a few days to accept or reject an offer.

There are many issues to consider when assessing a job offer.
Will the organization be a good place to work?

- Will the job be interesting?
- Are there opportunities for advancement?
- Is the salary fair?
- Does the employer offer good benefits?
- Now is the time to ask the potential employer about these issues—and to do some checking on your own?

The organization.

Background information on an organization can help you to decide whether it is a good place for you to work. Factors to consider include the organization's business or activity, financial condition, age, size, and location.

You generally can get background information on an organization, particularly a large organization, on its Internet site or by telephoning its public relations office. A public company's annual report to the stockholders tells about its corporate philosophy, history, products or services, goals, and financial status. Most government agencies can furnish reports that describe their programs and missions. Press releases, company newsletters or magazines, and recruitment brochures also can be useful. Ask the organization for any other items that might interest a prospective employee. If possible, speak to current or former employees of the organization.

Background information on the organization may be available at your public or school library. If you cannot get an annual report, check the library for reference directories that may provide basic facts about the company, such as earnings, products and services, and number of employees. Some directories widely available in libraries either in print or as online databases include:

- Dun & Bradstreet's Million Dollar Directory
- Standard and Poor's Register of Corporations
- Mergent's Industrial Review (formerly Moody's Industrial Manual)
- Thomas Register of American Manufacturers
- Ward's Business Directory

Stories about an organization in magazines and newspapers can tell a great deal about its successes, failures, and plans for the future. You can identify articles on a company by looking under its name in periodical or computerized indexes in libraries, or by using one of the Internet's search engines. However, it probably will not be useful to look back more than 2 or 3 years.

The library also may have government publications that present projections of growth for the industry in which the organization is classified. Long-term projections of employment and output for detailed industries, covering the entire U.S. economy, are developed by the Bureau of Labor Statistics and revised every 2 years. (See the Career Guide to Industries, online at www.bls.gov/oco/cg.) Trade magazines also may include articles on the trends for specific industries.

Career centers at colleges and universities often have information on employers that is not available in libraries. Ask a career center representative how to find out about a particular organization.

During your research consider the following questions:

- Does the organization's business or activity match your own interests and beliefs?
- It is easier to apply yourself to the work if you are enthusiastic about what the organization does.
- How will the size of the organization affect you?

Large firms generally offer a greater variety of training programs and career paths, more managerial levels for advancement, and better employee benefits than do small firms. Large employers also may have more advanced technologies. However, many jobs in large firms tend to be highly specialized.

Jobs in small firms may offer broader authority and responsibility, a closer working relationship with top management, and a chance to clearly see your contribution to the success of the organization.

Should you work for a relatively new organization or one that is well established?

New businesses have a high failure rate, but for many people, the excitement of helping to create a company and the potential for sharing in its success more than offset the risk of job loss. However, it may be just as exciting and rewarding to work for a young firm that already has a foothold on success.

The job

Even if everything else about the job is attractive, you will be unhappy if you dislike the day-to-day work. Determining in advance whether you will like the work may be difficult. However, the more you find out about the job before accepting or rejecting the offer, the more likely you are to make the right choice. Consider the following questions:

Where is the job located?

If the job is in another section of the country, you need to consider the cost of living, the availability of housing and transportation, and the quality of educational and recreational facilities in that section of the country. Even if the job location is in your area, you should consider the time and expense of commuting.

Does the work match your interests and make good use of your skills?

The duties and responsibilities of the job should be explained in enough detail to answer this question.

How important is the job to the company or organization?

An explanation of where you fit in the organization and how you are supposed to contribute to its overall goals should give you an idea of the job's importance.

What will the hours be?

Most jobs involve regular hours—for example, 40 hours a week, during the day, Monday through Friday. Other jobs require night, weekend, or holiday work. In addition, some jobs routinely require overtime to meet deadlines or sales or production goals, or to better serve customers. Consider the effect that the work hours will have on your personal life.

How long do most people who enter this job stay with the company?

High turnover can mean dissatisfaction with the nature of the work or something else about the job.

Opportunities offered by employers. A good job offers you opportunities to learn new skills, increase your earnings, and rise to positions of greater authority, responsibility, and prestige. A lack of opportunities can dampen interest in the work and result in frustration and boredom.

The company should have a training plan for you.

What valuable new skills does the company plan to teach you?

The employer should give you some idea of promotion possibilities within the organization. What is the next step on the career ladder? If you have to wait for a job to become vacant before you can be promoted, how long does this usually take? When opportunities for advancement do arise, will you compete with applicants from outside the company? Can you apply for jobs for which you qualify elsewhere within the organization, or are mobility within the firm limited?

Salaries and benefits.

When an employer makes a job offer, information about earnings and benefits are usually included. You will want to research to determine if the offer is fair. If you choose to negotiate for higher pay and better benefits, objective research will help you strengthen your case.

You should also look for additional information, specifically tailored to your job offer and circumstances. Try to find family, friends, or acquaintances that recently were hired in similar jobs. Ask your teachers and the staff in placement offices about starting pay for graduates with your qualifications. Help-wanted ads in newspapers sometimes give salary ranges for similar positions. Check the library or your school's career center for salary surveys such as those conducted by the National Association of Colleges and Employers or various professional associations.

If you are considering the salary and benefits for a job in another geographic area, make allowances for differences in the cost of living, which may be significantly higher in a large metropolitan area than in a smaller city, town, or rural area.

You also should learn the organization's policy regarding overtime. Depending on the job, you may or may not be exempt from laws requiring the employer to compensate you for overtime. Find out how many hours you will be expected to work each week and whether you receive overtime pay or compensatory time off for working more than the specified number of hours in a week.

Also take into account that the starting salary is just that—the start. Your salary should be reviewed on a regular basis; many organizations do it every year. How much can you expect to earn after 1, 2, or 3 or more years? An employer cannot be specific about the amount of pay if it includes commissions and bonuses.

Benefits also can add a lot to your base pay, but they vary widely. Find out exactly what the benefit package includes and how much of the cost you must bear.

WHAT TO EXPECT FROM THE OTHER SIDE OF THE TABLE...

HIRING THE BEST CCNP Routing and Switching

This chapter is all about clarity of the total hiring process – for you, your manager and your candidates.

You will need or encounter a Great Process to Hire the Best. Computers and equipment are wonderful tools, but people make the difference. Hiring the Best makes it clear just how valuable it is to hire and work with the best. The mistakes you will avoid make the investment very valuable. Hiring the Best provides you with a process that reduces trial and error in recruiting a lot, but still ensures that you will be able to hire the best.

This chapter guides you to how to perform a truly in-depth hiring process and interview for candidates. The process will allow you and your company to select the best candidates for key positions.

You will be able to use the materials shown here as an outstanding tool, giving you insight into the candidates experience, performance history, and growth allowing you to determine what they are capable of today and in the future.

This will, in short, let you go from hoping your next hire works out to being confident your next hire will be a star.

Before you make your next hire, use this Guide.

THE INTERVIEW AND SELECTION PROCESS

A position description, observing the job being performed, and interviewing the previous and current holders of the job and the immediate supervisor will be helpful in determining the competencies required and the performance standard.

Asking a series of questions will help you in establishing the technical competencies. Ask questions such as:

- What would the "perfect" candidate's competencies and skills look like;
- What will a person in this job have to do on a regular basis to

succeed;

- What are the necessary competencies and skills the person will need in order to achieve the desired results of the position;
- How will a person hired for this job know he or she is succeeding, and
- Why have people left this job in the past?

After you have analyzed the job and developed several technical competencies, list the top five most important technical competencies the candidate MUST have to succeed in the job.

Remember when developing your interview questions to keep the questions open-ended, simple, direct and specific. Base all the questions on the role its top five technical competencies.

Avoid questions that require overly specific knowledge.

Below is a sample Technical Competency Assessment Guide for use in determining the technical competencies and developing relevant interview questions.

Step 1

Technical Competencies Assessment Guide

Job Title: ________________________________

1. Analyze Technical Aspects of Job. (Answer questions and list competencies in the space.)

- What would the "perfect" candidate's competencies and skills look like?
- What will a person in this job have to do on a regular basis to succeed?
- What are the necessary competencies and skills the person will need in order to achieve the desired results of the position?
- How will a person hired for this job know he or she is succeeding?
- Why have people left this job in the past?

2. List the top five most important technical competencies the candidate MUST have to succeed in the job.

    1.

    2.

    3.

    4.

    5.

3. Develop a Technical Question for Each of the Five Required Technical Competencies.

- Base all your questions on the technical competencies you listed above.
- Keep the questions open-ended, simple, direct and specific.
- Avoid questions that require a specific knowledge of your division.
- Ask for assistance developing technical questions if you are not the technical expert.

Step 2

Determine the Customer Service Focused Competencies of the Job

A large percentage of employees who did not succeed in a position had the technical skills but did not have the customer service focused skills required for the job. Identifying the customer service focused competencies needed to successfully perform the job and determining if the candidate possesses those competencies is critical. For example, an individual working in a receptionist position will need to be flexible and unflappable in order to handle the pressure of multiple phone calls and simultaneous visitors. They also need some degree of friendliness for welcoming the public and some degree of extroversion, since most people calling an organization would like to be met by someone with enthusiasm.

Assessing customer service focused competencies during the interview process is something we may not be typically used to doing as managers. We are experienced in determining if the candidate has the technical skills and abilities to perform the job. But in order to get the BEST candidate for the position, customer service focused competencies need to be determined and assessed also.

To determine what customer service focused competencies are needed for the position, questions similar to those asked to determine the technical competencies should be answered:

- What would the "perfect" candidate's customer service focused competencies look like;
- What will a person in this job have to do on a regular basis to succeed;
- What are the necessary customer service focused competencies the person will need in order to achieve the desired results of the position;
- How will a person hired for this job know he or she is meeting the customer service focused expectations; and
- Related to customer service reasons, why have people left this job in the past?

As you think about the job vacancy you need to fill, focus on the customer service focused competencies or behaviors that an individual needs to exhibit in order to succeed in this job. Depending on the specific job under consideration, customer service focused characteristics, such as paying attention to detail, being self-motivated, getting along with others, having leadership qualities, and being tolerant of stressful events, are examples of the skills critical to success on the job.

Below you will find five descriptive elements of personality to assist you in determining customer service focused competencies. Descriptive words have been added to give you ideas and help you determine what behaviors are required for the position.

Towards the end of this document, you will find a list of questions to correspond to each personality factor. These questions can be used to develop the examination portion of the recruiting announcement or they can be used in the interview process.

The five descriptive elements of personality are Responsible, Likeable, Believable, Outgoing and Unflappable.

Definitions:

Responsible.

The ability to organize or schedule people, tasks, and self; to develop realistic action plans while remaining sensitive to time constraints and resource availability; and having a well developed sense of ethics and integrity. Characterized by high levels of responsibility and behaviors these employees are controlled, disciplined, precise, persistent, and businesslike. Their behavior is consistent, scrupulous, and reliable, and their work is purposeful, highly systematic, and well organized. They approach life as a series of tasks to be accomplished and goals to be reached.

Descriptors: detail-oriented; quality-focused; high-integrity; responsible; trustworthy; dependable; cost-conscious; exact; disciplined; committed; cautious; casual; easygoing.

Likeable.

Describes a person's ability to modify their behavioral style to respond to the needs of others while maintaining one's own objectives and sense of dignity. In the moderate to high range of likeability, we find sympathetic, helpful, and understanding individuals. They are agreeable, compassionate, thoughtful, and kind. They appear to accept things as they are, nurture others, and are obviously friendly and caring people.

Descriptors: amicable; accommodating; supportive; helpful; compromising; collaborative; friendly; empathetic; empowering; congenial; easygoing.

Believable.

Capable of eliciting belief or trust. In the middle to low range of believable thinking, we find people who are open, willing to reexamine tenets and consider new ideas. They are capable of reasonable levels of professional and personal risk taking and are willing to work outside their "comfort zone." Highly believable people can be described as practical, predictable and conventional, willing to follow procedures without question. They often form the emotional "back bone" of an organization.

Descriptors: creative; original; flexible; spontaneous; open-to-new-ideas; independent; curious; untraditional; venturesome; uninhibited; conventional; down-to-earth; concrete; traditional; practical; methodical; systematic.

Outgoing.

Describes the ability to work with people in such a manner as to build high morale and group commitments to goals and objectives. Individuals in the moderately high range of extroversion are upbeat, positive, and energetic. They tend to be enterprising, cheerful, and appropriately assertive. They demonstrate leadership, team-building capability, and are able to coach or facilitate a work team's progress. Individuals who are moderately introverted are often viewed as self-contained, generally well balanced, and able to work well either alone or in small groups.

Descriptors: active; outgoing; dominant; forceful; enthusiastic; assertive; persuasive; energizing; entrepreneurial; ambitious; risk-taking; self-contained; task-oriented; quiet; restrained; formal; unassuming; reserved; thoughtful.

Unflappable.

The ability to maintain a mature, problem-solving attitude while dealing with a range of stressful conditions, such as interpersonal conflict, hazardous conditions, personal rejection, hostility, or time demands. At moderately high levels of stress tolerance we find relaxed, secure, and hardy individuals who are poised and adaptive in a wide range of situations. They are steady, realistic, self-reliant, and able to cope effectively across a wide range of situations and circumstances. They demonstrate maturity that is not necessarily related to age, but to the ability to maintain a clear perspective under stressful conditions as well as those that elicit little or no stress.

Descriptors: calm; well adjusted; secure; even-tempered; self-assured; unflappable; resilient; poised; composed; self-confident; optimistic.

CUSTOMER SERVICE FOCUSED BEHAVIORS ASSESSMENT GUIDE

Job Title: ______________________________

A. List the most typical Customer Service Focused behaviors required on this job on a daily basis. Use the previously identified personality factors to help you.

- Responsible – detail-oriented; quality-focused; high-integrity; responsible; trustworthy; dependable; cost conscious; exact; disciplined; committed; cautious; casual; easygoing.
- Likeable – amicable; accommodating; supportive; helpful; compromising; collaborative; friendly; empathetic; empowering; congenial; easygoing.
- Believable – creative; original; flexible; spontaneous; open-to-new-ideas; independent; curious; untraditional; venturesome; uninhibited; conventional; down-to-earth; concrete; traditional; practical; methodical; systematic.
- Outgoing – active; outgoing; dominant; forceful; enthusiastic; assertive; persuasive; energizing; entrepreneurial; ambitious; risk-taking; self-contained; task-oriented; quiet; restrained; formal; unassuming; reserved; thoughtful.
- Unflappable – calm; well-adjusted; secure; even-tempered; self-assured; unflappable; resilient; poised; composed; self-confident; optimistic.

B. List of Customer Service Focused Behaviors

1.

2.

3.

4.

5.

C. Develop a Question for Each of the Customer Service Focused Behaviors

1.

2.

3.

4.

5.

Step 3

Develop Interview Questions to Assess Both Technical and Customer Service Focused Competencies

Decide how long the interviews will be and select a reasonable number of questions to ask. In a half-hour interview, only about 5 behavioral-based questions can comfortably be asked. If five questions are asked, at least two of them should be customer service-type questions, depending upon the type of job.

Always ask open-ended questions. Ask, "This job involves dealing with difficult customers. Think of a time when you had to deal with a difficult customer and tell us what you did." Don't ask, "Have you ever dealt with difficult customers?" You probably will get an answer like, "Yes, I work with difficult customers all the time." But it won't tell you HOW the individual works with difficult customers. If you feel the candidate is making up an answer, or is giving you a "canned" answer, ask a probing question or two to get more detail. "What exactly did you say to the customer to get them to stop yelling?" Generally, if they have read a book on "most commonly asked interview questions" and memorized an answer, or are making up the situation, a probing question will generally fluster them and they will not be as confident in giving an answer. You can ask for the candidate to think of another example to use in answering the question.

Using the list of most important tasks you developed during the review of the Position Description, develop open-ended questions to determine if the candidate has the technical skills necessary for the job. Only ask technical questions that relate to that particular job. Don't ask a question about using equipment if they don't use that equipment to do their job.

Using the list of customer service focused skills you identified from the position description are needed to do the job, develop open-ended questions to determine the candidate's customer service focused competencies.

There is a list of sample interview questions at the end of this document to help you.

They are arranged by the five personality factors identified above.

Step 4

Conducting the Interview

Have an interview panel of at least two managers/supervisors; some managers may also wish to include a non-management employee with special knowledge of the position duties as part of a panel.

If you choose to include a non-management employee on your interview panel, be sure to discuss interviewing procedures and confidentiality of candidate information with the employee prior to the interviews. It is encouraged that all interview panels be as diverse as possible.

Before the interview starts, establish the criteria used for scoring and then meet with the interview panel to discuss the process and review the questions and criteria used for scoring.

Welcome the candidate and establish rapport by introducing them to the members of the interview panel. Ask easy questions such as "Did you have any difficulty finding the office?" or "Would you like a glass of water before we begin?" Give a brief explanation of the organization or section and show the organization chart so they understand how this position fits within the organization. If you have handed the position description and organization chart out while they waited for the interview to start, ask if they have any questions

about the position or organization.
Explaining the interview process can also help ease a candidate's nervousness and also gives them information about the process, including, approximate length of the interview, the interview will be a series of prepared questions asked by the interview panel designed to get to know the candidate, and the panel will be taking notes during the interview.

Transition into the main purpose of the interview by saying, "Let's get a bit more focused and start asking the interview questions." Even though the interview process is accomplished through a panel, one person should act as "facilitator" and make sure the interview stays focused. Some candidates tend to wander, give "canned" speeches, or simply try to deliver a monologue. In such cases, you need to diplomatically interrupt and redirect the candidate to the question at hand. You might simply say, "I think we've gotten a little off target here. Let me restate my question."

To clarify a response or to get a candidate to give specific examples you can ask, "Please give me a specific example about when you..."
Because behavior-based questions require specific examples to answer them successfully, sometimes a candidate will need to think for a few seconds to come up with an appropriate example. You may have to wait 30, 60, or even 90 seconds for the candidate to start answering the question. Resist the temptation to talk during this silence! It takes time to recall specific behavioral examples that clearly answer your questions and you want the candidate to do their best during the interview. An option available to the hiring manager is to hand out the list of questions to the candidates a few minutes before the interview starts, so the candidate can start thinking of specific examples ahead of time and organizing their thoughts.

If an answer does not give you the information you need to rate the candidate's answer, use open-ended probes such as:

"Could you review your role in...?"
"Please describe how you..."
"What happened after...?"

If after the first or second try to get an answer more relevant to the question move on to the next question.
After each interview take a few minutes for the panel members to

summarize their thoughts and score the questions, or complete the rating process.

Affirmative Action

Organizations value diversity in the workplace. Every effort will be made to reach out to the broadest possible labor market. All employment decisions will be based on the most suitable candidate relative to a position, while taking into consideration Affirmative Action goals.

Step 5

Background and Reference Checks

The final stage of the hiring process is the background and reference checks. The Human Resources Background Investigator will verify information provided by the applicant by contacting former and current supervisors, persons listed by the candidate as references, and others who are thought to be able to provide information about the competencies of a candidate.

The Background Investigator listens for subtle innuendoes and long pauses after posing questions, and will evaluate whether the individual giving the reference sounds like he/she is struggling to carefully select each word. In these instances, more specific probing questions will be asked.

Occasionally, a finalist will indicate they do not wish you to contact their current employer. In these cases, you need to explain that the organization needs to contact this employer to assist with the hiring decision and that we don't hire anyone without completing a background and reference check with the current employer.

Making a Job Offer

When you have identified the candidate to whom you would like to make a job offer based on the information gathered through the application, examination, interview, evaluation of background and references, and you have the approval of your supervisor, and the Director or Deputy Director, you may contact that candidate and offer him/her the position.

Before you contact the candidate, please work closely with Human Resources staff to verify certain information. For example,

- Classification
- Salary Range
- Rate of pay and timing of first pay increase
- Vacation accrual rate and ability to transfer vacation accruals from another State organization
- Trial Service period
- Eligibility for Personal benefits

Confirming Job Offer Letter

Human Resources staff will send a confirming job offer letter. The letter will outline the terms of the job offer and will provide a space for the candidate to sign his or her name confirming that he/ she accepts the terms of employment. This signed copy must be returned to Human Resources to document the understanding and the acceptance of the terms.

It is important that all information in this letter of confirming letter of hire be correctly stated because it is an implied employment contract.

Informing Unsuccessful Candidates

After the selected candidate formally accepts your job offer, each of the remaining candidates should be contacted to notify them that the hiring decision has been made. Human Resources can help you with this step.

If a candidate contacts you directly to ask why he or she was not hired, the best thing to do is to simply tell them that we hired the most suitable candidate for the position. If they continue to ask for information, contact your Human Resources staff for guidance in how to answer the candidate's questions.

Retention of Interview Materials

Please collect all interview and selection materials and notes and return them promptly to Human Resources.

SAMPLE CUSTOMER SERVICE FOCUSED INTERVIEW QUESTIONS

(Grouped by customer service based behaviors)

Responsible

1. Tell us about a time when the details of something you were doing were especially important. How did you attend to them?
2. Describe a time when you had to make a difficult decision on the job. What facts did you consider? How long did it take you to make a decision?
3. Jobs differ in the extent to which people work independently or as part of a team. Tell us about a time when you worked independently.
4. It is often easy to blur the distinction between confidential information and public knowledge. Have you ever been faced with this dilemma? What did you do?
5. Tell us about a time when you put in some extra effort to help move a particular project forward. How did you do it and what happened?
6. Tell us about a demanding situation in which you managed to remain calm and composed. What did you do and what was the outcome?
7. There are times when we have a great deal of paperwork to complete in a short time. How do you do to ensure your accuracy?
8. Give an example of a time you noticed a process or task that was not being done correctly. How did you discover or come to notice it, and what did you do?
9. We often have to push ourselves harder to reach a target. Give us a specific example of when you had to give yourself that extra push.
10. Tell us about a time when you achieved success through your willingness to react quickly.
11. Tell us about a time when you disagreed with a procedure or policy instituted by management. What was your reaction and how did you implement the procedure or policy?
12. What kinds of measures have you taken to make sure all of the small details of a project or assignment were done? Please give a specific example.
13. How do you determine what constitutes a top priority in

scheduling your work? Give a specific example.

14. If I call your references, what will they say about you?
15. What are two or three examples of tasks that you do not particularly enjoy doing? Tell us how you remain motivated to complete those tasks.
16. What has been your greatest success, personally or professionally?
17. What can you tell us about yourself that you feel is unique and makes you the best candidate for this position?
18. What strengths do you have that we haven't talked about?
19. Tell us about a time when you had to review detailed reports or documents to identify a problem. How did you go about it? What did you do when you discovered a problem?
20. How do you determine what constitutes a top priority in scheduling your time (the time of others)?
21. Do you have a system for organizing your own work area? Tell us how that system helped you on the job.
22. Have you planned any conferences, workshops or retreats? What steps did you take to plan the event?

Likeable

1. Tell us about a time when you were able to build a successful relationship with a difficult person.
2. Give us an example of how you have been able to develop a close, positive relationship with one of your customers.
3. Give us an example of how you establish an atmosphere at work where others feel comfortable in communicating their ideas, feelings and concerns.
4. Describe a particularly trying customer complaint or resistance you had to handle. How did you react and what was the outcome?
5. How would you describe your management style? How do you think your subordinates perceive you?
6. Some people are difficult to work with. Tell us about a time when you encountered such a person. How did you handle it?
7. In working with people, we find that what works with one person does not work with another. Therefore, we have to be flexible in our style of relating to others. Give us a specific example of when you had to vary your work style with a particular individual. How did it work out?
8. It is important to remain composed at work and to maintain a positive outlook. Give us a specific example of when you were

able to do this.

9. Having an understanding of the other person's perspective is crucial in dealing with customers. Give us an example of a time when you achieved success through attaining insight into the other person's perspective.
10. Have you ever had difficulty getting along with a co-worker? How did you handle the situation and what was the outcome?
11. Tell us about a time when you needed someone's cooperation to complete a task and the person was uncooperative. What did you do? What was the outcome?
12. There are times when people need extra assistance with difficult projects. Give us an example of when you offered assistance to someone with whom you worked.
13. Tell us about a situation in which you became frustrated or impatient when dealing with a coworker. What did you do? What was the outcome?
14. Many jobs are team-oriented where a work group is the key to success. Give us an example of a time when you worked on a team to complete a project. How did it work? What was the outcome?
15. Tell us about a job where the atmosphere was the easiest for you to get along and function well. Describe the qualities of that work environment.
16. On occasion we may be faced with a situation that has escalated to become a confrontation. If you have had such an experience, tell me how you handled it. What was the outcome? Would you do anything differently today?
17. Describe a time when you weren't sure what a customer wanted. How did you handle the situation?
18. We don't always make decisions that everyone agrees with. Give us an example of an unpopular decision you have made. How did you communicate the decision and what was the outcome?

Believable

1. Describe your ideal supervisor.
2. What were some of the most important things you accomplished on your last job?
3. What is your management style? How do you think your subordinates perceive you?
4. Give us an example of when someone brought you a new idea, particularly one that was odd or unusual. What did you do?

5. It is important that performance and other personnel issues be addressed timely. Give examples of the type of personnel issues you've confronted and how you addressed them. Including examples of the process you used for any disciplinary action taken or grievance resolved.
6. Give us an example of how you establish an atmosphere at work where others feel comfortable in communicating their ideas, feelings and concerns.
7. Give a specific example of how you have involved subordinates in identifying performance goals and expectations.
8. All jobs have their frustrations and problems. Describe some specific tasks or conditions that have been frustrating to you. Why were they frustrating and what did you do?
9. Jobs differ in the degree to which unexpected changes can disrupt daily responsibilities. Tell what you did and us about a time when this happened.
10. What are your standards of success in your job and how do you know when you are successful?
11. Sometimes supervisors' evaluations differ from our own. What did you do about it?
12. What do you do differently from other (__________)? Why? Give examples.
13. We don't always make decisions that everyone agrees with. Give us an example of an unpopular decision you made. How did you communicate the decision and what was the outcome?
14. Describe a situation in which you received a new procedure or instructions with which you disagreed. What did you do?
15. Describe a situation in which you had to translate a broad or general directive from superiors into individual performance expectations. How did you do this and what were the results?
16. Give an example of how you monitor the progress your employees are making on projects or tasks you delegated.

Outgoing

1. Describe a time when you were able to effectively communicate a difficult or unpleasant idea to a superior.
2. Tell us about a time when you had to motivate a group of people to get an important job done. What did you do, what was the outcome?
3. Tell us about a time when you delayed responding to a situation until you had time to review the facts, even though there was

pressure to act quickly.

4. There are times when we need to insist on doing something a certain way. Give us the details surrounding a situation when you had to insist on doing something "your way". What was the outcome?
5. On occasion, we have to be firm and assertive in order to achieve a desired result. Tell us about a time when you had to do that.
6. Being successful is hard work. Tell us about a specific achievement when you had to work especially hard to attain the success you desired.
7. In job situations you may be pulled in many different directions at once. Tell us about a time when you had to respond to this type of situation. How did you manage yourself?
8. Many of us have had co-workers or managers who tested our patience. Tell us about a time when you restrained yourself to avoid conflict with a co-worker or supervisor. (restrained)
9. In working with people, we find that what works with one person does not work with another. Therefore, we have to be flexible in our style of relating to others. Give us a specific example of when you had to vary your work style with a particular individual. How did it work out?
10. Describe some particularly trying customer complaints or resistance you have had to handle. How did you react? What was the outcome?
11. Have you ever had difficulty getting along with co-workers? How did you handle the situation and what was the outcome?
12. Tell us about a time when you needed someone's cooperation to complete a task and the person was uncooperative. What did you do? What was the outcome?
13. Tell us about a situation in which you became frustrated or impatient when dealing with a coworker. What did you do? What was the outcome?
14. Sooner or later we all have to deal with a customer who has unreasonable demands. Think of a time when you had to handle unreasonable requests. What did you do and what was the outcome?
15. Tell us about a time when you were effective in handling a customer complaint. Why were you effective? What was the outcome?
16. How do you know if your customers are satisfied?

Unflappable

1. There are times when we all have to deal with deadlines and it can be stressful. Tell us about a time when you felt pressured at work and how you coped with it.
2. Give us an example of a demanding situation when you were able to maintain your composure while others got upset.
3. On occasion, we experience conflict with our superiors. Describe such a situation and tell us how you handled the conflict. What was the outcome?
4. We have to find ways to tolerate and work with difficult people. Tell us about a time when you have done this.
5. Many times, a job requires you to quickly shift your attention from one task to the next. Tell us about a time at work when you had to change focus onto another task. What was the outcome?
6. Tell us about a time when you received accurate, negative feedback by a co-worker, boss, or customer. How did you handle the evaluation? How did it affect your work?
7. Give us an example of when you felt overly sensitive to feedback or criticism. How did you handle your feelings?
8. Give us an example of when you made a presentation to an uninterested or hostile audience. How did it turn out?
9. Tell us about a time when you put in some extra effort to help move a project forward. How did you do that? What happened?
10. Describe suggestions you have made to improve work procedures. How did it turn out?

INTERVIEWING CCNP Routing and Switching

A Practical Guide for Selecting

THE INTERVIEW PROCESS

Planning

Time spent planning will ensure the interview process proceeds smoothly and that you obtain the information needed to assess the candidates. You should:

- Review the position description and qualification requirements (refer to the vacancy announcement).
- Thoroughly review all candidate applications. Ask yourself: – What are the strengths/weaknesses of this candidate?
- What is the candidate's relevant skills/experience? – Does the education fit the job requirements?
- Is there evidence of the ability to communicate with individuals and groups from diverse backgrounds in a variety of situations?
- Is there evidence of the ability to lead and accomplish work through others?
- Decide who you will interview. Although you are not required to interview all candidates, think about the perception of other candidates if you interview only one person.
- Formulate questions and write them down. This will help ensure you ask all candidates the same questions.
- Allow 1-2 hours for the interview.
-

Confirming/Scheduling Interview

Selecting officials are encouraged to confirm scheduled interviews with applicants in writing.

Conducting the Interview

After welcoming the candidate, spend a few minutes chatting informally. It will help you both relax.

- Give a brief overview of the job and mission of the organization.
- Ask questions and listen.
- Probe for additional information. Ask the candidate to elaborate on or clarify what was just said. (Although it is important that you write down a list of questions before you begin the interviews, you are not prohibited from asking additional questions.)
-

Indirect probing is also an effective way to elicit more information. If you are silent for a few seconds after the candidate responds, that may allow them time to think of additional things to say; or you may use neutral phrases, such as: I see, or, oh? That may prompt the candidate to elaborate further. The point is that in this phase of the interview, it is the candidate who should be doing most of the talking.

- Take notes, but don't try to capture every word. It's distracting to you and the candidate.
- Allow the candidate time to ask questions. This is where you can elaborate on the Organization, your lab, and/or the specific job.
- Inform the candidate about maxi flex, leave, benefits, holidays, etc.
-

Some suggested interview questions can be found in TIPS ON INTERVIEWING.

Closing

If the candidate won't be considered further, close the interview diplomatically. If you are interested in the candidate, you may:

- Ask if the candidate is still interested in the position.
- Inform the candidate of the next step. Be prepared to advice on the timeframe for selection and how the selectee will be notified.
- Inform the candidate that references will be checked.
- Thank the candidate for coming for the interview, applying for the position, and/or having an interest in the Organization and position.
- Write up your notes.
-

Follow Up

A good customer service practice is to write all candidates acknowledging the interview and thanking the person for showing an interest in the organization. You may wish to do so after a selection has been made.

TIPS ON INTERVIEWING

Questions/ Assessment Tools

Careful thought should be given to constructing the interview.

Together with the KSAs (knowledge, skills, and abilities) and SPFs (selective placement factors) you used in the vacancy announcement, the kind of questions you ask will determine the type of person you select for your position. There are various assessment tools available to evaluate candidates including:

A. The Behavioral Event Inventory (BEI). The candidate describes, in detail, a past experience that demonstrates the KSA or competency to a panel. The panel is facilitated by a person trained in the method. The phases of the process include planning, orientation, and interviewing, debriefing, and follow-up documentation.

B. The Traditional Interview. Questions are developed prior to the interview. The same basic questions are asked of each candidate. Additionally the interviewer can,

- Encourage the candidate to give an example of a real situation, activity, or problem that includes: a description of the context, or environment; evidence or characteristics of the audience; the action taken; and the outcome.
- Ask open-ended questions. Asking yes and no questions will severely limit the kind of information you obtain from the interview. The only yes or no question you should ask is, "Are you still interested in this position?"
-

Interview Questions To Get You Started

- What interests you most about our position?
- What role do you take in a group situation? Give an example.
- Why do you want to work for our organization?
- What are your short-term and long-term goals?
- What are the two biggest accomplishments in your life?
- What has been your greatest technical achievement in your current position? Your career?
- Describe your participation in professional associations.
- What planning processes have you found useful? In what way do you feel you have improved in your planning abilities/ methods?
- How does your past experience impact your qualifications for this position?
-

Supervisor and Manager Competencies

When preparing for supervisory or managerial interviews (whether using traditional or BEI), all candidates must be evaluated using the following two competencies:

A. Leading People. This competency includes conflict management, cultural awareness, team building, mentoring, and integrity/honesty (either work related or outside experience). Ask each candidate to describe a situation, problem, or event that demonstrates:

- Ability to work with a diverse group.
- Ability to prevent or mediate a conflict or disagreement or overcome dissension in a group.
- Ability to instill trust and confidence in others.
- Use of skills and abilities as a leader under stressful conditions.
-

B. Building Coalitions/Communications. This competency includes oral and/or written communication, influencing/negotiating, partnering, interpersonal skills, and political savvy. Ask each candidate to describe a situation, problem or event that demonstrates:

- Ability to express ideas or give instructions not easily or readily understood by their audience.
- Ability to make presentations to groups in order to gain acceptance of an idea by the group.
- Negotiating skills to gain approval for change or modification to programs, procedures, etc.
-

Interviewing People With Disabilities

Concentrate on the applicant's technical and professional knowledge, skills, abilities, experiences and interests, not on the disability. Remember, you cannot interview a disability, hire a disability or supervise a disability. You can interview a person, hire a person, and supervise a person.

The American with Disabilities Act (ADA) separates the hiring process into three stages: pre-offer, post-offer and employment. At each stage, the rules differ regarding the permissibility of disability-related questions and medical examinations. Definition of a "Disability-Related Question" means a question that is likely to elicit information about the disability. Definition of "Medical Examination" is a procedure or test that seeks information about an individual's physical or mental impairments or health.

Therefore, the two most important questions for employers to address are:

- Is the question disability-related or is the examination medical? And
- Where are we (i.e., at which stage - pre-offer, post-offer, or employment) in the employment process?
-

At the first stage (the pre-offer stage), the ADA prohibits all disability-related questions and medical examinations, even if the questions or examinations are related to the job. At the second stage (after the applicant is given a conditional job offer), the law allows all disability-related questions and medical examinations, as long as all entering employees in the job category are asked the questions or given the examinations. At the third stage (after the employee starts work), the law permits disability-related questions and medical examinations only if they are job-related and consistent with business necessity.

The law requires that medical information collected at any stage must be kept confidential.

For examples of some commonly asked questions on "Pre-employment Disability - Related Questions and Medical Examination Questions," please refer to the Equal Employment Opportunity Commission website at www.eeoc.gov/docs/preemp.html.

Accommodating Persons With Disabilities For An Interview

- Application and interviewing procedures should comply with the American with Disabilities Act (ADA). The ADA prohibits disability-related questions or medical exams before a real job offer is made.
- Agencies employment offices and interviewing location(s) are to be accessible to applicants with mobility, visual, hearing or cognitive disabilities.
- Be willing to make appropriate and reasonable accommodations to enable a job applicant with a disability to present him or herself in the best possible light. When setting up the interview explain what the hiring process involves

and ask the individual if he or she will need reasonable accommodations for any part of the interview process. For example, if a person who is blind states he or she will need help filling out forms, provide the assistance; provide an interpreter for an applicant who is deaf, if he or she requests one; provide details or specific instructions to applicants with cognitive disabilities, if this type of accommodation is required.

- Do not let a rehabilitation counselor, social worker or other third party take an active part in or sit in on an interview unless the applicant requests it.
- Make sure that all questions asked during the interview are job-related. Speak to essential job functions regarding the position for which the applicant is applying, as well as why, how, where, when and by whom each task or operation is performed. Do not ask whether or not the individual needs an accommodation to perform these functions, because such information is likely to reveal whether or not the individual has a disability. This is an ADA requirement to ensure that an applicant with a disability in not excluded before a real job offer is made.
-

Interview Do's and Don'ts

DO...

- Be friendly to establish rapport, help the candidate feel at ease.
- Listen attentively.
- Keep the interview under control. If the interviewee becomes verbose or drifts off the subject, it's your job to get back on track.
- Use professional terminology to evaluate the candidate's knowledge.
- Consider potential as well as current ability.
- Note the kinds of questions the candidate asks. Do they concern opportunities for self-improvement and increased responsibilities, or only pay and fringe benefits?
- Be objective. Know yourself and your stereotypes.
- Understand that we tend to hire people who look like us.
- Be honest, even if it means saying something negative (e.g., the facility is old and there is not much office space). Just don't overemphasize it.
- Observe the candidate.
- Relax and enjoy the interview.
-

DON'T...

- Talk too much.
- Use a rigid or overly standardized approach. If you've prepared your questions, you can be flexible during the interview, knowing that you can easily get back on track. You'll become more flexible and react easily to different situations and personalities as you gain experience.
- Try to impress the interviewee with your knowledge.
- Hide demands of the job. A good candidate reacts favorably to these.
- Make commitments you may regret or are not authorized to make.
- Be satisfied with surface facts. Look for reasons, and probe.
- Take detailed notes. It may keep you from observing nonverbal responses and maintaining the conversational flow.
- Ask questions in a way that indicates the answers you want.
- Ask convoluted or over-defined questions.
- Be aggressive or evasive.
- Raise candidates' hopes when they are not likely to be selected.
-

CHECKING REFERENCES

You have completed the interviews, but you are not done yet.

A resume and interview are great tools, but the reference check is really the only way you have to verify information given by the candidates.

Normally, you will conduct a reference check on the one or two finalists. Reliability of the reference check is based on the concept that past performance is a good predictor of future performance. Reference checks will help:

- Verify information the candidate provided both in the application and during the interview.
- You gain insight into who your candidates are and how they behave in the workplace.
-

Never make an offer (remember, you can only make a tentative offer) without first doing an exhaustive check of the candidate's background. A comprehensive reference check goes back 5 years and includes contacting a minimum of three sources that are knowledgeable about the candidate's abilities. Contact

Enough references to confirm the quality of your selection.

Which References Should I Check?

- Academic references–institutions and teachers/professors.
- Current and former supervisors–immediate supervisors are often the best sources for reliable information about a candidate's work performance.
- Your network of professional associates/associations.
- Candidate's personal references–they will generally provide a favorable reference. Ask them for names and positions of other persons who know the candidate and contact them.
- Candidate's colleagues–business or work associates will sometimes provide an objective analysis of the candidate's strengths and weaknesses.
- Seek your own independent sources who know the candidate.
-

Tips for Checking References

- Ask only job-related questions and ask the same questions about each candidate.
- Ask open-ended questions and probe.
- Use telephone reference checks rather than mail inquiries since they are faster and less time consuming.
- Keep the conversation casual. If you speak to the person in a relaxed manner, you will get better results.
- If the reference provider keeps talking, keep listening and asking more questions. Seek out judgmental comments and try to read between the lines of what the person is telling you. A reference who says the candidate tried hard or is a people person may be saying such things to avoid talking about real problems or issues.
- Do not eliminate one candidate because of poor references and then neglect to check references from the remaining candidate(s).
- Always check dates and times the person giving the reference worked with or supervised the candidate, and then
- Determine if there is a personal relationship.
- Give only a general description of the vacant position. Too many details may bias the reference person in formulating their

answers. As in the case of the employment interview, let the other person do most of the talking.

- Do not use leading questions such as "He's a good manager, isn't he?"
- Do not let a prominent characteristic, such as a good academic record; overshadow less obvious or possibly negative traits, such as a poor leave record.
- Speak to someone in addition to the current supervisor. A dishonest supervisor may try to unload a problem employee by giving a glowing reference.
- Listen carefully to the answers you are given and take notes.
-

The Reference Check Questions To Ask

When contacting a reference, we recommend you begin with,

"Thank you for taking a few moments to provide information about our job candidate. The information you provide will be considered along with other information submitted by the applicant and other references. Please be aware that under the Federal government's employment policies, we may become obligated to disclose the information to the applicant or others involved in the selection or review process."

Then, ask and record the answers to the following:

- How long have you known the candidate?
- In what capacity were you associated with the candidate? As employer? Supervisor? Co-worker? Friend? Other?
- Using a scale of 1-5, with 1 being poor and 5 being excellent, how would you rate the candidate in comparison to most others you have known.
-

	RATINGS 1 2 3 4 5
Work ethic?	________
Work quality?	________
Technical skills?	________
Writing skills?	________
Communication skills?	________
Interpersonal skills?	________
Reliability & dependability?	________
Receptivity to feedback?	________

Adaptability to change? ________
Ability to deal with job stress? ________

- What would you consider to be some of this candidate's most positive attributes or strengths?
- What would you consider to be some areas where this person is not as strong or needs to improve?
- What type of work environment does the candidate require to excel?
- Describe the candidate's initiative, personality, and negative habits.
- How does the candidate get along with customers? Co-workers? Supervisors and managers?
- Is the candidate reliable? Honest? Trustworthy? Of good character?
- Would you rehire the candidate?
- Is there any other information concerning the candidate's qualifications, character, conduct and general fitness I should know about?
-

Prohibited Questions and Practices

- Please do not put yourself in a position of engaging in a prohibited personnel practice related to employment and selection. As a selecting official with the authority to take, direct others to take, recommend, or approve any personnel action, you must not:
- Discriminate for or against any employee or candidate for employment on the basis of race, color, national origin, gender, religion, age, disability, political beliefs, sexual orientation, and marital or family status.
- Deceive or willfully obstruct any person with respect to such person's right to compete for employment.
- Influence any person to withdraw from competition for any position for the purpose of improving or injuring the prospects of any other person for employment.
- Appoint or employ a relative to a position over which you exercise jurisdiction or control as a selecting official.
- Take or fail to take a personnel action with respect to a candidate for employment as a reprisal.
- Discriminate for or against a candidate for employment on the basis of conduct which does not adversely affect the performance of the candidate or the performance of others

(except for criminal behavior).

•

RECORDING A PROFILE OF IMPRESSIONS

Candidate's Name______________________

1. What are the candidate's strongest assets in relation to the requirements for this position?
2. What are the candidate's shortcomings in relation to this position?
3. The candidate seemed knowledgeable about/ interested in:
4. Contradictions or inconsistencies noted were:
5. The candidate was evasive about:
6. Overall, the candidate responded to questions with: (e.g., openness, confidence, poise, directness, glibness, evasiveness, etc.) Examples?
7. Overall, reference checks were positive, mediocre, less than positive. Examples/key descriptions or characteristics?
8.

Supervisory and Managerial Competencies:

Leading People is there evidence demonstrating:

1. Ability to gain commitment and support from others?
2. Ability to develop solutions to management problems?
3. Ability to establish performance objectives?
4. Ability to foster cooperative working environment among employees?
5. Ability to deal with morale and employee concerns?
6.

Building Coalitions/Communication:

Is there evidence demonstrating:

1. Conflict resolution?
2. Working as a member of a team?
3. Expression of ideas and views that others understand and that influence (persuade) them to act?
4.

RECRUITING CCNP ROUTING AND

SWITCHING - IT TAKES MORE THAN A JOB ANNOUNCEMENT

Job searcher - here is the recruiter's perspective on the placement process, written from the perspective of the recruiter, the full inside scoop, to enable you to know what is going on begind the scenes and prepare for it.

One of the critical steps in the recruitment process involves the actions you take to speed up the process and reach the largest, desirable pool of candidates.

Simply posting the vacancy on job websites will not guarantee that you receive quality applications for the job. This chapter provides suggestions on steps YOU should take to ensure YOUR recruitment activity works for YOU.

Considering these suggestions can help minimize the time required for recruitment on YOUR end and also help the Human Resources (HR) Specialist speed up the process.

Before Submitting the Vacancy

Review and rethink the position description

- Ensure that the duties and responsibilities reflect the needs (or discipline) of the position at this time.
- Determine if it accurately reflects the knowledge, skills, and abilities (KSAs) needed to perform the job.
- Ensure that the KSAs can be directly related back to duties and responsibilities in the position description.
- Develop your "Quality Experience" definition. Identify experience a candidate will need to bring to the job on day one.

Consider alternative hiring methods

- Determine if the position can be filled using the Student Career Experience Program (SCEP), Federal Career Intern Program, Career Enhancement Program, and USDA Direct Hire Authority, special hiring authorities for individuals with disabilities or veterans, or other hiring methods.

Think about the vacancy announcement

- Determine who the applicants are you are trying to reach.
- Determine if you will need to recruit nationwide or if there will be sufficient candidates in the local commuting area to give you a diverse applicant pool from which to select.

Develop a strategy to reach your candidate

- Identify ways to market the job announcement to reach potential applicants.
- Visit or contact the Career Center, Deans, and Professors if you are located on a campus to promote and highlight the many career opportunities available with ARS.
- Identify colleagues (both within and outside the organization) who can help in marketing the job.
- Identify colleges and universities or professional societies and organizations where the announcement should be mailed.
- Identify newspapers, journals, or online advertising sites that might be useful in marketing the job.
- Contact the Recruitment Office and your Area Civil Rights Manager for ideas on how to reach a diverse candidate pool.

Contact your servicing HR Specialist

- Discuss recruitment strategies and alternatives, as well as expectations for completion of the action.
- Keep in touch with your HR Specialist by e-mail during the recruitment process.

Submit all required paperwork

- Submit all position descriptions and forms needed to request the personnel action.
- Submit draft ad text along with the request to save time (remember, your servicing HR Specialist must review and approve all ads prior to being placed).
- Submit your "Quality Experience" definition.

When the Vacancy Announcement is Open

Conduct your Marketing

- Be PROACTIVE!
- Personally identify potential candidates and send a note with the announcement or call to encourage them to apply – be cautious, however, and don't give the impression they will get the job.
- Send the vacancy announcement to individuals, schools and

colleges, or organizations you have identified, and place ads in newspapers, magazines, and online job boards.
- E-mail the announcement to co-workers, colleagues, stakeholders, and peers with a brief note asking for assistance in publicizing the job.
- Document your efforts.

Identify a Diverse Group of Interview Panel Members and Set Up Panel Dates

- Ask your HR Specialist for an approximate timeframe for receipt of the certificate of eligibles.
- Ask interview panel members to block out time on their calendars for the interview process.
- Clear your calendar also!
- Keep your interview panel members informed throughout the recruitment process – if conflicts arise, replace panel members immediately.

Develop Interview Questions

- Share interview questions with the panel members for comments and suggestions.

Contact Your HR Specialist Throughout The Process

- Ask if you are receiving applications.
- Determine if you need to extend the closing date. Ask your HR Specialist to scan applications received to get an idea of the quality of applicants before making a decision to extend the closing date.

Once the Certificate of Eligibles is Received

Schedule the Interviews Immediately So The Best Candidates Are Still Available

- Review the certificate right away and identify the candidates you believe should be interviewed. Ask for help from colleagues as needed. Set a timeframe to complete the interviews.
- Schedule the interviews close together to minimize losing a desirable candidate and to maximize the likelihood of remembering individual candidates' strengths and weaknesses.
- Have an open mind – interview "Preference Eligible" (Veterans and Displaced) candidates before making judgments on their ability to do the job. Remember, if they are on the certificate, they meet the qualifications for the position. Talk to your HR

Specialist if you have concerns.
- Advise applicants of your timeframe for conducting the interviews – if they are interested, they will make themselves available.
- Advise the candidates of the process you will use to conduct interviews (for example, interview panel – give them guidelines).

Conduct Reference Check
- Always conduct reference checks on top candidates! This is more critical than ever before.

Make Your Tentative Selection
- Contact the candidate selected to advise that their name is being recommended to Human Resources. Ask if any issues with pay, incentives, EOD, etc.
- Notify HR Specialist of your decision and discuss options for offering recruitment incentives. Remember, the HR Specialist must make the official offer of employment.
- Obtain required area/organization approvals of the selection and incentives being proposed.
- Ask the HR Specialist to issue the written employment offer including information on negotiated pay, recruitment incentives and bonuses, and EOD date.

After The Selection is Made

Notify other candidates interviewed of your decision
- HR will notify all non-selected candidates of the final outcome.
- Contact the candidates interviewed and encourage them to apply for other positions.

Share impressive applications
- Share other impressive applications with colleagues who may be recruiting for similar jobs – they can contact and encourage quality applicants to apply for their positions.
- Share a copy of other impressive applications with the Recruitment Office – this office can refer the applications to others recruiting for similar positions.

Prepare for the new employee/s arrival
- Make copies of appropriate policies, procedures, and other documents the new employee should read.
- Have the employee's workspace cleaned up and the desk

stocked with essential supplies.
- Prepare the performance plan and provide it along with a copy of the position description on the first day of work.
- Set time on your calendar to spend with the new employee on the first day – show them around the facility, discuss the job and work they will be doing, provide time to read through materials, and let the employee know they can ask questions.
- Make sure the employee is set up with an e-mail address and computer access, etc.
- Identify a mentor and develop an Individual Development Plan (IDP) to address with the employee.
- Inform the employee of the probationary period requirements as well as the promotion potential, if any, of the position.

ASSESSING YOUR RECRUITMENT AND SELECTION PRACTICES

Policies and Procedures

This completes your view from the other side of the table, the recruiters' - and helps you in understanding their workload and point of view.

Your organization's policies and procedures should thoroughly document the recruitment, assessment and selection processes.

The policies and procedures should be accessible and understood by not only HR professionals but Managers and others involved in the hiring process.

Ask yourself these questions to help assess whether or not your organization's policies and procedures are current and include new requirements.

- Are recruitment, assessment and selection processes supported by written policies and procedures that are up-to-date, accurate and complete? (Ideally within 2 years.)
- How widely communicated are the organization's written recruitment, assessment and selection policies to those who are involved in the process? (Ideally to all staff.)
- Does the organization utilize these policies and procedures for the recruitment, assessment and selection processes?

- Does the organization have a written policy describing procedures for the review of competencies and/or qualifications?
- Does the organization follow a formal recruitment, assessment and selection plan at the start of each recruitment? (Link to sample recruitment plan)
- Training Managers, supervisors, and personnel involved in the hiring process should receive comprehensive training in the organization's full recruitment process and thoroughly understand proper interview and selection techniques.
- Who performs recruitment activities for the organization? (Ideally HR with unit management participation.)
- On average, how long does it take to fill a position within the organization from the start of recruitment until an offer is extended? (Ideally 2 months or less.)
- Does the organization provide training and/or written guidelines about recruitment, assessment and selection policies and procedures to managers and supervisors prior to them seeking to fill a position (e.g., reviewing applications, conducting interviews, and evaluating candidates)?

Recruitment Strategies

The organization should tailor their recruitment strategy to meet the need for the specific position and the organization's goals, as well as attract a diverse pool of applicants.
Does the organization develop a specific recruiting and marketing plan to identify how and who they need to contact to help achieve finding the best candidates?

- Does the organization have a plan to recruit qualified applicants who represent the diversity of the State or local service area?
- Does the organization compare its workforce demographics to the State, county or local labor force demographics?
- Does the organization utilize specialized recruitment strategies to attract hard-to-find, qualified candidates?
- What recruitment strategies are utilized to attract hard-to-find qualified candidates? (Ideally executive search firms, internet job sites, local and regional newspapers, job fairs, professional organizations, civic organizations, networking, Employment Security Department, etc.)
- Does the organization track the effectiveness of different recruiting methods?

- Are recruitment sources periodically evaluated to assure they meet the needs of the organization and return on investment calculated?

Recruitment Process and Hiring

- Recruitment procedures should be developed and administered in compliance with all applicable organization policies, bargaining agreements, laws, regulations, and professional standards.
- Is a job analysis conducted to identify the key responsibilities of a position prior to announcement?
- Are required qualifications reviewed prior to position announcements to assure they are job related?
- Are preferred qualifications reviewed prior to position announcements to assure they are job related?
- Does the organization's HR staff assure all applicants selected for employment meet the posted qualifications for the position?
- What percentage of job announcements identify the competencies needed to perform the job?
- Are essential functions of the position discussed with the candidate?
- Does the organization utilize a behavioral interviewing tool to develop standardized, relevant interview questions?

Selection Process

- Selection procedures should be developed and administered in compliance with all applicable laws, regulations, and professional standards.
- What methods are used for the selection process? (Ideally selection matrix, interview notes, resume ranking, skills testing, reference checks, background checks, etc.)
- What percentage of the final selection decisions is documented? (This includes reasons for hire versus non-hire.)
- How long is the selection documentation retained?
- Does the organization evaluate and assess how well the selection procedures worked?
- How frequently does the organization assess its selection procedures?
- Does the organization maintain documentation of the assessment process?

Glossary

A

Annual: recurring, done, or performed every year; yearly

Applicant: a person who formally applies for a job

Apprenticeship: a formal relationship between the worker and sponsor that consists of a combination of on-the-job training and related occupation-specific instruction. Apprenticeship programs usually provide at least 144 hours of occupation-specific technical instruction and 2,000 hours of on-the-job training per year over a 3- to 5-year period. Apprenticeships are associated mostly with the trades. Examples of occupations that utilize apprenticeships are electricians and structural iron and steel workers; see On-the-job training

Associate's degree: degree awarded usually for at least 2 years of full-time academic study beyond high school; see Education

Average: the quantity calculated by adding a set of numbers and dividing the resulting sum by the quantity of numbers summed; see Mean

B

Bachelor's degree: degree awarded usually for at least 4 years of full-time academic study beyond high school; see Education

Base year: year used as a reference point for comparison with later years. For example, 2010 is the base year for the 2010–2020 employment projections. Employment in the base year is actual 2010 data, whereas employment in the target, or projection, year is projected

Business cycle: The periods of growth and decline in an economy. There are four stages in the cycle: expansion, when the economy grows; peak, the high point of an expansion; contraction, when the economy slows down; and trough, the low point of a contraction

Baby-boom generation: individuals born between 1946 and 1964

C

Certification: award for demonstrating competency in a skill or set of skills, typically through the passage of an examination, work experience, training, or some combination thereof. Certification is always voluntary. Some certification programs may require a certain level of educational achievement for eligibility.

Consolidation: the merger of two or more commercial interests or corporations

Current Population Survey (CPS): a national survey that samples 60,000 households on a monthly basis and collects information on labor force characteristics of the U.S. civilian noninstitutional population; the CPS is conducted by the Census Bureau for the Bureau of Labor Statistics

D

Demand for workers: total job openings resulting from employment growth and the need to replace workers who leave jobs

Doctoral or professional degree: degree awarded usually for at least 3 years of full-time academic work beyond a bachelor's degree; for example, some science and other occupations need a doctoral degree, and all lawyers, physicians, and dentists need a professional degree for employment; see Education

Domestic sourcing: moving jobs to lower cost regions of the United States instead of to other countries

Duties: the major tasks or activities that employees in an occupation usually perform

E

Earnings: Pay or wages of a worker or group of workers for services performed during a specific period—for example, hourly, daily, weekly, or annually. Also see Pay, Wages

Education: levels of education typically needed for entry into an occupation are classified as follows:

Doctoral or professional degree: degree awarded usually for at least 3 years of full-time academic work beyond a bachelor's degree; e.g., lawyers, physicians and surgeons, and dentists

Master's degree: degree awarded usually for 1 or 2 years of full-time academic study beyond a bachelor's degree

Bachelor's degree: degree awarded usually for at least 4 years of full-time academic study beyond high school

Associate's degree: degree awarded usually for at least 2 years of full-time academic study beyond high school

Postsecondary nondegree award: usually a certificate or other award that is not a degree. Certifications issued by professional organizations or certifying bodies are not included in this category. Programs may last only a few weeks to 2 years. e.g., nursing aides, EMTs and paramedics, and hairstylists

Some college, no degree: a high school diploma or the equivalent, plus the completion of one or more postsecondary courses that did not result in any degree or award

High school diploma or equivalent: the completion of high school or the equivalent resulting in the award of a high school diploma or the equivalent, such as the General Education Development (GED) credential

Less than high school: the completion of any level of primary or secondary education that did not result in the awarding of a high school diploma or the equivalent

Employment growth/shrinkage: increase or decrease in the number of jobs

Entry level: the starting level for workers who are new to an occupation; different occupations may require different levels of education, training, or experience upon entry

Employed: the situation of a person who has an agreement with an employer to work full time, part time, or on a contractual basis for that employer

Employment: the number of jobs in an occupation, including full-time, part-time, and self-employed. For example, employment of accountants and auditors was 1,216,900 in 2010

F

Fieldwork: an investigation or search for material, data, etc., made in the field as opposed to the classroom, the laboratory, or official headquarters. For example, archeologists working at a dig site in the desert; historians or curators finding or collecting artifacts for museums; and environmental technicians collecting water samples from a pond, a stream, or an ocean

Fixed work schedules: schedules of employees who work the same hours on an ongoing basis—for example, 9 a.m.–5p.m.; see Work schedules

Flexible work schedules: schedules of employees who set their own hours within specified guidelines and with a fixed number of total hours; see Work schedules

Full time: 35 hours or more per week, according to the Current Population Survey; see Work schedules

G

GDP (gross domestic product): the market value of all final goods and services produced within a country in a given period; the most commonly used measure of the size of the overall economy. The Bureau of Economic Analysis (BEA) produces estimates of GDP.

GED (General Educational Development): a credential signifying the completion of a program that is equivalent to a high school curriculum; see Education

Greater than full time: more than 40 hours per week; see Work schedules

Growth rate: the percent change in the number of jobs added or lost in a U.S. occupation or industry over a given projection period; see "Information Found in the Occupational Outlook Handbook"; growth rate adjectives used in the OOH are defined by the following percent changes for the 2010–20 employment projections:

much faster than the average: 29 percent or more
faster than the average: 20 percent to 28 percent
as fast as the average: 10 percent to 19 percent
more slowly than the average: 3 percent to 9 percent
little or no change: –2 percent to 2 percent
decline moderately: –3 percent to –9 percent
decline rapidly: –10 percent or less

H

High school diploma or equivalent: award or credential that is equivalent to a high school diploma, such as a high school diploma itself or the General Educational Development (GED) credential;

see Education

Household: all persons who occupy a housing unit

I

Important qualities: characteristics and personality traits that are likely needed for workers to be successful in given occupations

Industry: a group of establishments that produce similar products or provide similar services; see NAICS

Internship: training under supervision in a professional setting. This category does not include internships that are suggested for advancement; see On-the-job training

Injury and illness rate: ratio expressing the number of workers sustaining a wound, strain, or infection due to an incident or exposure at the workplace per 100 workers; the Occupational Safety and Health Administration (OSHA) considers an injury or illness to be work related if an event or exposure in the work environment either caused or contributed to the resulting condition or significantly aggravated a preexisting condition; in general, a Handbook profile will cite an injury and illness rate only if it is particularly high compared with the rate for all other occupations

J

Job openings: job openings occur when occupations grow, creating new jobs, and when workers leave an occupation permanently, resulting in the need to replace them

Job: a specific instance of employment; a position of employment to be filled at an establishment; see Employment

Job outlook: a statement that conveys the projected rate of growth or decline in employment in an occupation over the next 10 years; also compares the projected growth rate with that projected for all other occupations; Also see growth rate

Job prospects: a qualitative measure of the competition for jobs that takes into consideration factors such as the growth or decline in numbers of jobs, the expected number of qualified workers, and/or the expected number of applicants; a comparison of the number of jobs with the number of potential workers and jobseekers

K

No entries

L

Labor force: the sum of all persons 16 years and older in the civilian noninstitutional population who are either employed, or unemployed but available for work and actively looking for work

Less than high school: the completion of any level of primary or secondary education that did not result in the awarding of a high school diploma or the equivalent; see Education

Less than 1 year (of work experience in a related occupation): the level of experience in another occupation typically needed for entry into a given occupation; see Required training for entry; also Work experience in a related occupation

Long-term on-the-job training: more than 12 months of on-the-job training or programs not including apprenticeships; see On-the-job training

Licenses: permission granted by government agencies or other accrediting bodies that allows for the selling of certain goods or services

M

Master's degree: degree awarded usually for 1 or 2 years of full-time academic study beyond a bachelor's degree; see Education

Mean: the mathematical average of a set of numbers, calculated by adding the numbers and dividing the total by the number of numbers summed; see Average

Median: the middle number in an ordered list of numbers

Moderate-term on-the-job training: 1 to 12 months of on-the-job training or programs, not including apprenticeships; see On-the-job training

More than 5 years (of work experience in a related occupation): the number of years of experience in a related occupation typically needed for entry into a given occupation; see Required training for entry; also Work experience in a related occupation

N

North American Industry Classification System (NAICS): Industry classification system used by federal statistical agencies in classifying business establishments for the purpose of collecting, analyzing, and publishing statistical data related to the U.S. economy

New job: an addition of a position to an establishment's payroll, usually as a result of economic expansion

Nonfixed work schedules: schedules of employees who work different hours on one job; often used to accommodate particular traits of individual workers or because the work required by the employers varies for each individual; see Work schedules

None (on-the-job training): the situation when no additional occupation-specific training or preparation is typically required to attain competency in an occupation; see On-the-job training

None (required training for entry): the situation when no work experience in a related occupation is typically required to enter a given occupation; see Required training for entry; also Work experience in a related occupation

Number of jobs: number of actual instances of employment according to the BLS National Employment Matrix; see the projection methods page for more information about the Matrix

Numeric change in employment: a projected change in the number of jobs in an occupation or industry

O

On-the-job training: training or preparation that is typically needed, once employed in an occupation, to attain competency in the occupation. Training is occupation specific rather than job specific; skills learned can be transferred to another job in the same occupation

Internship/Residency: training under supervision in a professional setting. This category does not include internships that are suggested for advancement.

Apprenticeship: a formal relationship between a worker and his or her sponsor that consists of a combination of on-the-job training and related occupation-specific instruction. Apprenticeship programs usually provide at least 144 hours of occupation-specific technical instruction and 2,000 hours of on-the-job training per year over a 3-to-5-year period. Apprenticeships are associated mostly with the trades. Examples of occupations that utilize apprenticeships include electricians and structural iron and steel workers.

Long-term on-the-job training: more than 12 months of on-the-job training or programs, not including apprenticeships.

Moderate-term on-the-job training: 1 to 12 months of combined on-the-job experience and informal training

Short-term on-the-job training: 1 month or less of combined on-the-job experience and informal training

None: no additional occupation-specific training or preparation

Occupation: a craft, trade, profession, or other means of earning a living. Also, a set of activities or tasks that employees are paid to perform and that together go by a certain name. Employees who are in the same occupation perform essentially the same tasks, whether or not they work in the same industry

P

Pay: Earnings or wages of a worker or a group of workers for services performed during a specific period—for example, hourly, daily, weekly, or annually. Also see Earnings, Wages

Part time: less than 35 hours of work per week, according to the Current Population Survey; see Work schedules

Percent: one part in a hundred. For example, 62 percent (also written 62%) means 62 parts out of 100

Percentile wage estimate: the value of a wage below which a certain percentage of workers fall

Percent change in employment: growth rates expressed as percentages

Personal consumption: total goods and services purchased

by individuals in the U.S. economy; the amount of goods and services used or purchased by individuals or households in the U.S. economy; a key statistic in measuring or calculating overall GDP

Population: The total number of inhabitants of the United States

Postsecondary nondegree award: a certificate or other credential that is awarded by an educational institution upon completion of formal postsecondary schooling. (The postsecondary nondegree certificate is different from certifications issued by professional organizations or certifying bodies.) Postsecondary nondegree award programs may last from just a few weeks to 2 years. Examples of those who need postsecondary nondegree awards are nursing aides, emergency medical technicians, and hairstylists ; see Education

Q

Qualifications: personality traits, education, training, work experience, or other qualities workers need to enter an occupation

Important qualities: characteristics and personality traits that are likely needed for workers to be successful in given occupations

R

Related occupations: occupations that have similar job duties; see Similar occupations

Replacement rate: the rate at which workers permanently leave the occupations in which they are employed; large occupations that have high replacement rates need many workers to fill jobs that are vacated.

Replacement needs: the number of projected openings expected to result from workers who retire or permanently leave an occupation; replacement needs are calculated from monthly CPS data

Residency: training under supervision in a professional setting. This category does not include internships that are suggested for advancement; see On-the-job training

Rotating work schedules: schedules that have a fixed number of hours and time off over a period of more than 1 week, but not a set weekly schedule, according to data from the 2010 Current

Population Survey; see Work schedules

S

Salary: earnings of a worker or a group of workers for services performed during a specific period—for example, an hourly straight-time wage rate or, for workers not paid on an hourly basis, straight-time earnings divided by hours worked

Seasonal employment: employment that is not expected to last a full year, but that may reoccur; for example, many retail sales associates are hired only for the busy holiday season, and forest firefighters are more likely to be employed during the summer months, when vegetation is dryer

Short-term on-the-job training: 1 month or less of on-the-job experience and informal training; see On-the-job training

Similar occupations: occupations that tend to share common daily tasks or require similar skill sets, rather than similar wages or education

Self-employed: those who work for profit or fees in their own business, profession, trade, or farm; only the unincorporated self-employed are included in the self-employed category

SOC code: the Standard Occupational Classification (SOC) system, which is used by all federal statistical agencies to classify workers into occupational categories for the purpose of collecting, calculating, or disseminating data

Some college, no degree: a high school diploma or equivalent, plus the completion of one or more postsecondary courses that did not result in a degree or award; see Education

Supply of workers: the number of people in the labor force; for most occupations, the supply of workers is smaller than the total number in the labor force because the supply is limited to those with particular education or training requirements

T

Training: see On-the-job training; or Required training for entry; or Work experience in a related occupation

U

Undergraduate degree: Bachelor's degree; see Education

Union membership: the group of workers who join labor unions, hold union memberships, and enjoy benefits of the organized, coordinated efforts of the union to improve the work environment

V

Vocational school: a secondary school that teaches vocational trades, such as construction trades; vocational schools may or may not award degrees; see Education

W

Wage: earnings or pay of a worker or a group of workers for services performed during a specific period—for example, hourly, daily, weekly, or annually. Also see Earnings, Pay

Work schedules: the number of daily hours, weekly hours, and annual weeks that employees in an occupation are scheduled to, and do, work. Short-term fluctuations and one-time events are not considered unless the change becomes permanent; for more details, visit Work Schedules in the National Compensation Survey

Fixed work schedules: schedules under which employees who work those schedules do so on an ongoing basis; e.g., 9 a.m.–5 p.m.

Flexible work schedules: schedules under which employees set their own hours within guidelines and with a fixed number of total hours

Rotating work schedules: schedules that have a fixed number of hours and time off over a period of more than 1 week, but not a set weekly schedule

Nonfixed work schedules: schedules of employees who work different hours on one job; often utilized to accommodate particular traits of individual workers or because the work required varies by individual

Greater than full time: more than 40 hours per week

Full time: between 35 and 40 hours of work per week

Part time: Less than 35 hours of work per week

Work experience in a related occupation: the level of work

experience in an occupation related to a given occupation; may be a typical method of entry into the given occupation

X, Y, Z
No entries

19694231R00066

Made in the USA
Lexington, KY
02 January 2013